Malvern in a Day

Malvern in a Day

Life in the early 1970s through the photographs of Michael Dowty and the memories of local people

Jan Condon

Malvern in a Day
Jan Condon

Published by Aspect Design, 2023
Designed, printed and bound by Aspect Design
89 Newtown Road, Malvern, Worcs. WR14 1PD
United Kingdom
Tel: 01684 561567
E-mail: allan@aspect-design.net
Website: www.aspect-design.net

A copy of this book has been deposited
with the British Library Board.

Cover image: Girls and Buses (D075)

ISBN 978-1-912078-26-4

Contents

Introduction

Welcome to *Malvern in a Day*. The book reflects aspects of life in and around 1971, the year in which Michael Dowty took the set of photographs which he called *Malvern in a Day*. I have based the contents primarily on his photographs, all taken on 30 July 1971, and on people's memories and contributions to the oral history project, many of which cover a wider time frame but add to Malvern's social history.

The initial project to catalogue and conserve the photographs which are held in Malvern Library is part of a wider and longer-term project of cataloguing and conservation of historic items being carried out by the Friends of Malvern Museum. For the book I have also added material from research into local and social history from published and on-line information sources. A major aid to the project has been Goad's Plan which you can read about in the Sources of Information section at the end of the book.

Michael Dowty and the Photographs

If you had been out and about in Malvern Link just after six o'clock on the morning of Friday 30 July 1971, you may have seen a man with a camera taking the first of many photographs. Few people were around at that time of day. The man with camera was Michael Dowty.

Michael was a professional photographer from Worcester and a frequent visitor to Malvern. At the request of the Librarian, he took the 202 black and white photographs of Malvern 'from dawn to dusk'. The photographs were handed over to the library, some were displayed and recently the collection has been digitized. The photographs have been removed from their original box and folders, which were unsuitable for long term storage, and are now in archive standard sleeves and boxes for safe keeping and reference use at the library. Michael listed his photos and gave them numbers and titles, some of them quirky, others the names of shops, premises, and streets. He had produced an 'in a day' series for Worcester, possibly in response to a national newspaper article on the destruction of some of Worcester's old buildings. He photographed the city on Saturday 3 August 1968, from 6.15 am to 9.00 pm. The photographs were displayed locally and published twenty years later.

In an earlier book he celebrated the work of his photographer father William Ward Dowty (1887–1979) who had established his photography business in Worcester at 8 Broad Street where Michael grew up. William

Illus. 1. Michael Dowty

Ward Dowty was born in Pershore where his father, William, had bought a chemists shop to which he successfully added photography, renaming the shop Rembrandt House. There is a commemorative plaque opposite Pershore Heritage Centre where you can see an interesting display about the Dowty family. Michael's Worcester photographs are located in the Worcestershire Archives at the Hive in Worcester. His observations and decisions on what to photograph in Malvern on one day in 1971 have provided the town with a unique record of aspects of its life at that brief moment in time.

Michael Dowty died suddenly aged sixty-eight in 1999.

The Fifty-first Anniversary of the Photographs

I was not able to prepare and produce an exhibition to celebrate the fiftieth anniversary of the photographs in 2021 because of Covid restrictions. However, despite the rain on 30 July that year, several Malvern Civic Society members turned out to photograph Malvern fifty years on to the day. Their contributions, *A Day in Malvern*, will be catalogued and added to the archived collection. A year later, however, with the essential input of Ian Thompson Photography, and help and financial support from several individuals and organizations, and, importantly, with cooperation from the Dowty family who own the copyright to the photographs, with my colleague Rosemary Preece, I designed an exhibition for July and August 2022 which showed off some of the photographs on posters displayed outside Waitrose and Wilko in Church Walk. Some of the posters included short quotations from the people of Malvern who had shared their memories with us. The posters and the photographs are now available to view in Malvern Library.

It was impossible to count those who visited the exhibition but from comments received and from occasional observation, hundreds looked at, enjoyed, and talked about what they saw. This book came about because of their enquiries and the positive response the exhibition produced.

The Book

It could be argued that 1971, was a year of considerable change. The local newspaper of the time, the *Malvern Gazette*, covered, for example, the introduction of decimal currency, the change to North Sea Gas, discussion about entry into the Common Market, possible changes to local government and the spread of comprehensive education.

For the purposes of organizing the contents of the book, I have not attempted to reconstruct Michael's route which varied as the day wore on. I have for the most part kept the contents focused on Great Malvern, partly for reasons of space but also because this is where most of the activity shown in the photographs is found. It has not, however, been possible to research or include all the places in Great Malvern. The photos

Illus. 2. Visitors to the exhibition, summer 2022

Illus. 3. Visitors to the exhibition, summer 2022

show aspects of a town captured as it appeared on the day. Nothing is posed, people are doing ordinary things and Michael Dowty chose to record some of them.

Some of the oral and written memories cover a much wider time frame but are relevant to the early seventies and its late sixties background. The earlier history of some businesses and places has also been included to illustrate other changes which have taken place over a longer period of time.

I hope that the selection photographs, contributions and comments on history and aspects of life in and around the early seventies will add further to our knowledge of the social history of the town.

Proceeds from the sale of the book will help to fund further work on conservation, research, and exploration of Malvern's history.

Chapter One
Shops and Shopping

Before reading about spending money and costs of items in the shops, it may be useful to have an idea of average earnings and to mention the two kinds of taxes which applied to businesses and retail – they occur from time to time in the advertisements on the photographs or in people's memories.

Men in manual jobs in 1970 earned on average £26-16s a week (£1,394 a year) at eighteen or over. In non-manual work (known as 'white collar') men earned £35-16s a week (£1,861 a year) at twenty-one or over. Women at eighteen or over in manual work earned £13-8s a week (£696 a year). In non-manual work earnings were £16.16s a week (£873 a year).

Taxes: Purchase tax was levied on the wholesale value of 'luxury' goods. Rates varied and depended on the decision of the government. It was reduced on 19 July 1971 – the first time since 1963. SET, Selective Employment Tax, was introduced in 1966 as a tax on businesses which did not boost exports, in effect, a tax on service industries. It was based on their weekly payroll (set at £2.40 on male employees, £1.20 on women).

It was halved from 5 July 1971. VAT replaced these taxes when Britain joined the Common Market.

Now to the shops. Great Malvern in the seventies had a wide variety of shops and businesses. Joy McWhirter told us of her impressions of the shopping facilities. She started with Lipton's:

> What was Lipton's like inside? It was self-service, if I remember rightly, and wasn't that big. There were a lot of varied shops. You wouldn't recognize even the corner where the traffic lights are now. We had a Courts furniture store which is now the Halifax; we had Burston's electrical shop which is now Rhubarb; we had Malvern Gentlemen's Club which is now the estate agent's and we had the Bank which is now going to be a 'destination venue', I think. And there were a lot of shops. We had hardware shops, pet shops, dress shops – all sorts of things.

(*Opposite page*) illus. 4. Brays (D006)

The Department Stores

BRAYS

Hubert Bray had a tailor's shop in Ledbury. In 1895 he leased what was number 1 the Promenade in Malvern for seven years. It had been built in the Italianate style in local brick between 1865 and completed 1867, with five shops on the ground floor. Hubert formed a partnership with his nephew Charles Davis who later acquired Hubert's share. The business expanded firstly to number 4 and later over the years the other

BRAYS
BRAYS
BRAYS
PROMENADE RESTAURANT
CAFE

shops were added. In 1956 Brays bought the freehold to the premises, enabling the business to knock through walls to join up access to the various departments they had developed.

Christopher Davis described Menswear at Brays.

> Having started work at Brays twelve years earlier with experience at first in the office and then in the downstairs Men's Department, in 1969 I moved upstairs to the Outerwear Department to work with John Grundy. He had many years experience with the firm, having started in 1928. Our territory was made up of the main large 'Showroom' as it was known, a smaller front room adjoining which contained antique styled rails of suits and jackets, and a back room which housed boys' wear – not just school uniform items but casual knitwear, shorts, trousers and dressing gowns as well. In fact, some of the schoolwear, mainly blazers, overflowed into the main Showroom.
>
> The transition to a more casual style of dress was only just developing, and although we had a short rail of golf and walking jackets by Windak and Grenfell (nearly all in a putty colour) the emphasis was still very much on formal suits, sports jackets and overcoats, both full length and in the shorter 'car coat' style. Trousers were either in grey or a heather mixture by Daks or in fawn cavalry twill from Bladen. Men's jeans, as far as Brays were concerned, were unheard of . . .
>
> There were by now no longer any tailoring staff on the premises and alterations were sent out to one or two ladies working at home, the deliveries

and collections being made by Bill Pratt, a shop porter, on one of the two delivery days each week.

The knitwear stock included lambswool pullovers (V and crew neck), slipovers and cardigans mainly from Cox Moore, whose range also included a very popular knitted waistcoat. Heavier weight sweaters came from Kilspindie and Alan Paine, and we also stocked Norwegian pullovers in traditional patterns which were very hard wearing. These were also in boys' sizes, being popular with parents as, over time, they tended to stretch rather than shrink, and so kept pace with the child growing.

The fixture behind the large counter was utilised for our stock of full-length raincoats, lighter weight coats by Driway contrasting with heavier self-lined coats from Grenfell.

Later on, this space was taken over by dressing gowns but when I first moved into the department the stock of wool gowns was kept in folded piles on the top of the tall fixtures.

Another activity in the department was hire wear from Moss Bros. for weddings and evening functions ... We now obtained the hire clothing through their Birmingham branch who delivered by van. Just occasionally if an item was needed urgently, they would send the box by Midland Red bus, which would sometimes mean an anxious vigil at the end window of the Showroom watching to see if the conductor of the next 144 double decker off loaded it at their office which was just across the road.

In February 1971, like all other businesses, Brays had to move over to decimal currency. Christopher Davis described staff preparation.

> We had to do some staff training beforehand and I think we got some training kits from our trade association. And I suppose we had about fifteen staff, something like that, in those days. And I remember having half the staff up into the office on a Monday morning and the other half on a Tuesday morning for half an hour. And we had about four or five sessions, I should think, practicing giving change with dummy money, and . . . how cheques should be written and so on.
>
> School wear, especially for the prep schools in the area, was a significant feature of Brays business from its early times in Malvern. The shop also supplied schools further afield. Other departments included Ladies fashion (which expanded further in 1990 to include lingerie and corsetry, following the closure of Marie in Church Street;) ready to wear suits and shoes (1949) and travel goods.) Although its telephone systems were updated, the old tills remained until 2020.

Brays announced its closure in August 2019. Christopher Davis, approaching the age of eighty, announced his retirement after more than sixty years in the business and his colleague Stuart Stone, who had been with the firm for forty-three years, most recently as managing director, was approaching retirement age. It was, declared the *Malvern Gazette*'s headline: 'The End of an Era'.

Local businessman Richard Simmonds acquired the premises. The building has been renovated and now houses the popular Faun's restaurant (from Church Street), Solo, an excellent selection of clothes and accessories, and the award-winning Austin's with Sean Austin's wide range of cards, stationery and gifts. Faun's bought some of the old shop fittings which have been re-purposed to provide display counters for food and drink. Malvern Civic Society has put up a commemorative plaque outside the former Brays store.

WARWICK HOUSE AND THE MAN'S SHOP

Sally Trepte contributed information in her memories about Warwick House. Its owner had been her grandmother Gertrude Mitchell who retired aged seventy-eight in 1959 and her father was later managing director. Sally gives a detailed picture of the business and its history in her recent book (see Bibliography for details).

In its day Warwick House attracted clients from all over the county and further a-field with its beautiful and fashionable clothes and formal wear. Its bridal service provided wedding dresses, bridesmaids dresses and could and did dress the relatives of the wedding party, if clients desired. Sally's book tells of the staff and their training, the attitude of Warwick House to quality, the range of clothes and accessories, the fitting and alterations service clients could expect and lots more. Here are a few extracts from her memories from the early 1970s around the

WARWICK HOUSE
MALVERN

(*Opposite page*) illus. 5. Warwick House
1.00 pm (D074)

time when Michael Dowty photographed the famous shop and its off shoot, The Man's Shop.

The sense I have of when Gertrude Mitchell Ltd amalgamated with Cox and Painters in 1943 and my Grandmother Gertrude Mitchell set about reorganizing and refurbishing Warwick House was that she wanted to do what she had done in her High Street, Worcester shop; that was, to create space. And so, my memory of Warwick House in Malvern as I was growing up and into the early Seventies was of a big sense of space. And a lot of that was to do with the high ceilings, certainly in the town end of the building. There was always the awareness to keep up to date with the fashion industry. Fashion trends changed. Less people were wearing hats, more people were wearing more casual clothes, in Warwick House terms 'separates'. There were decisions made to move departments round, while still retaining the spaciousness and calm air. I am not quite sure how that was carried out.

I think also at that time, the Warwick House restaurant was moved from Belle Vue Terrace, where Gallery 36 is, over to the only showroom in Warwick House on the lower ground floor, I think. So there was a sense of trying, despite the increased taxation, trying to change things in the hope of creating greater profits . . . That sense of space and calmness belied what was going on underneath. So, 1971, I can't remember when exactly SET came in, Selective Employment Tax, but I know that this was the beginning of a very, very difficult period for my father who was managing director,

Geoffrey Lampard. My grandmother retired in 1959 and he then became sole managing director.

Selective Employment Tax. What I was aware of was that some industries, and organizations got a rebate. Firms like Warwick House didn't, and I would say that that was the beginning of the end for our family business . . . keeping the building going, keeping heads above water financially with the building was always a headache. There was so much of it below ground which was up against the hill and there were constant issues with damp. There was also a large area right at the top of the building which wasn't used and so heat used to disappear up there. The upkeep of the building was a constant headache . . . I don't think many people really realized that.

Marcella Hales worked at Warwick House for a year before taking up her place at Birmingham University. What was it like?

Well, it was very attractive. The building was very nice and it had a sweeping staircase. And I remember Mrs Bell and her model gowns. She used to go up to London to buy twice a year and we were all excited to see what she bought when the delivery came, and we went and had a look. It was a grand place really. They had a Men's Department along the Terrace. And the Ladies, it was rather special. The workshops were at the top so you could have anything altered there and then, and the offices where I worked were downstairs and the technology was very basic . . . The phone was still the plug-in variety. And yes, it was a rather snobby place but had a lot of customers from a long way away. It did extremely well with the School Uniform Department. When I came, there were nine schools, private schools, and they all, you know . . . you had to get the uniform from that place. They did extremely well out of the schools locally.

Karen Hill spoke about her mother's visit to the café.

My mother and her friends used to make Friday morning their shopping morning . . . After a while these ladies would all meet up at one of the cafés . . . They went to Warwick House Café on Belle Vue Terrace which just had a doorway entrance in the middle of the Terrace and it was an L shaped interior building with no outside windows and had small wall lights that lit the room but it always seemed rather dark inside. Later on the Warwick House moved their café to the main building and sold the one on Belle Vue Terrace.

And Emma told us about her grandma's visits.

I used to go to Warwick House with my grandma when I was a little girl. Grandma liked Warwick House. It was a rather posh shop. She always dressed in her smartest clothes when she was going there. Grandad had a rather old car which, because it wasn't at all smart, grandma insisted should be parked well away from the shop. So we had to walk quite a way back to the entrance to it.

THE MAN'S SHOP

This was a rather neat, plain, double fronted shop. It was housed in premises over two floors bought by Warwick House in 1935 in part of the former Belle Vue Hotel. You can still see part of the hotel name with the word 'hotel' blanked out above the central part of Belle Vue Terrace today. Gertrude Mitchell, owner of Warwick House, and her husband already owned the shop and flat of number 32. The name 'The Man's Shop' says it all: it stocked all kinds of high-quality clothing for men. It also had a side window facing onto the 1930s arcade. Now it is called more exotically Iapetus (the name given to the sea between two ancient continents, called after a Titan in Greek mythology). The shop is well known today for its wide selection of interesting and beautifully crafted gifts and cards. In the arcade you can see the original art deco window glass and brass framing. The premises became Gieves and Hawkes in the 1980s and in the next decade was Gemma's Country Crafts then Fearnside Art Materials. The former restaurant was at one time Edward G's wine bar and more recently the Gallery 36 Restaurant. In 2022 it closed and has recently been sold.

The end of Warwick House? Warwick House itself was also sold to Gieves and Hawkes of Saville Row but the business was not successful. As Sally noted, the introduction of SET contributed to the end of the business. In 1993 a company, Warwick House Investments Ltd., was formed by businessmen with the purpose of turning Warwick House

Illus. 6. The Man's Shop (D197)

into apartments. Building started in October 2000 and finished in October 2008. The *Malvern Gazette* (14/11/2008) recorded that a month later the developer went into voluntary liquidation and the business was wound up. Creditors included a local builder and two estate agents. The sale of the premises was not affected and today the iconic building is still an interesting asset to the town.

Illus. 7. The Great Malvern Hotel leaflet (courtesy of the hotel)

KENDALL'S AND COURT'S

It seems rather strange to take a photograph showing hoardings round a building but this one was in a prominent position and indicates how Michael Dowty wanted to record the state of the town as it was, even though some of the things he saw were not particularly photogenic.

The corner of Graham Road and Church Street had once been the fine-looking entrance to the Beauchamp Hotel as shown on the photograph of the current interesting leaflet of its successor, the Great Malvern Hotel.

The Beauchamp was described as a Victorian coaching inn built in 1842. The area around the hotel would have been occupied by a garden growing fresh produce, and by stables and accommodation for its staff and servants of visitors. It was aimed at the emerging middle class rather than the well-off visitors, a 'family boarding house and commercial hotel'. On Michael Dowty's photograph you can see the windows of the original buildings. The hotel was reduced in size after

LENNARDS
TO CAR
PARK

(*Opposite page*) illus. 8. Church Street (D094)

the second world war. The corner is now taken up by the Halifax Bank. Its entrance is on Church Street rather than at the corner, with Costa Coffee and A-Plan Insurance (recently relocated from further down Church Street) next door.

For many years the end of the building was occupied by David Kendall who moved his shop from the other side of Church Street in 1854 into what became a shop joining the Hotel. Kendall's sold according to an 1858 account,

> mantles [coats], hats, blankets and sheets and unshrinkable undergarments and everything clients would need for hydropathic treatment.

Aimed at the middle market, it also stocked shoes, underwear, haberdashery, fashions and materials for knitting and sewing. Cash payments only were required and payments were taken on wires spinning above the counters. Over the years Kendall's, who had taken a partner, Mr J. Thompson, into the business in 1879, expanded their range and developed into a popular department store. The previous doorway to the hotel became an excellent site for a display window with the store entrance just up the street. Two of its customers who saw the Dowty photo in the 2022 exhibition remembered Kendall's well and recalled childhood visits.

There were wonderful displays of toys on the top floor and we made visits at Christmas time to Father Christmas who gave out real, as opposed to rubbish, presents.

Katharine Barber recalled,

In 1965 I started work as a secretary. I bought two suits from Kendall's. I liked the shop very much. I bought material for baby blankets in 1968.

The shop was in a very convenient location, especially for people living down the hill who could find a variety of goods they needed without venturing further up Church Street. Katharine remembered the effort required,

I remember pushing a Silver Cross pram up Church Street with baby and toddler on the baby seat. I was wearing a short skirt. The toddler had to walk down as the pram was heavy to restrain.

Mr G. Thompson, Kendall's partner's son, succeeded his father in the business and finally put it up for sale. The *Malvern Gazette* reported in April 1971.

Furnishing Company to buy Kendall's premises. The purchasers of the property vacant since last November are Court Bros (Furnishers) Ltd. A company with several branches throughout the country.

Courts expected to open as soon as planning approval to carry out alterations was obtained and the building was renovated. In June the headline in the *Gazette* was 'New Shop Front for Kendall's'.

As we can see from the photo, the work was continuing at the end of July. Courts presence was welcomed by one newcomer to Malvern in the early '70s. Joy McWhirter commented,

> You could furnish your dining room with a sideboard, table and chairs for £80.

The *Guardian* (29/11/2002) recorded that Courts Furniture suddenly closed its shops after 154 years of trading had ended with huge debts when the banks called in the receivers. Courts seem to have had a comparatively short life in Malvern and by 1990s the premises were occupied by the Halifax and Supersave toiletries and cosmetics.

WOOLWORTH'S, 24–26 CHURCH STREET

A man looking at this photograph asked,

> Was it once a cinema? . . . Of course it is Iceland now.

F. W. WOOLWORTH & Co. Ltd.
NEW! SHOPPING MADE EASY WITH CASH-WRAP SERVICE
Purchase Tax Cuts Immediate Reductions
TO CAR PARK
Winter Gardens Theatre – Cinema Information Bureau

(*Opposite page*) illus. 9. Woolworths (D085)

The cinema identification wasn't far off the mark. The building is in the art deco style commonly used for 1930s cinema buildings. But this was also the style used by Woolworths' in-house design team and used for several stores of the time. And with its red name sign, it was an instantly recognisable feature of many high streets. Built in 1935–36 with glazed ceramic decoration above the sign, the shop was a stylish addition to the Church Street prime site.

Woolworths first arrived in Britain from the US and opened in 1909 in Liverpool with a grand ceremony including fireworks and a circus . . . and queues of eager shoppers. Its business was to sell products everyone needed at affordable prices. At the time of this 1971 photograph, Woolworths in Malvern was still thriving. Although she shopped at other shops, especially Lipton's, Joy McWhirter also went to Woolworths.

> There were various other shops as well: there was a Co-op and a deli and I used to get my cheese in Woolworths. I don't know why, but they had a cheese counter inside.

Young Jane Shawyer had a summer job in Woolworths, first as a cleaner where she used

> one of those machines, wobba wobba machines we called it with the round things that cleaned the floors.

She then worked on Saturdays in the shop itself.

> As you walked into Woolworths on the left side was the old-fashioned cheese counter and as you went beyond that there was the pick-and-mix counter . . . to the right of the shop, there was a record counter as well.

With her sister she also worked on the check-out tills.

> We would sit on the tills and we would try our best to be in competition with each other to get people through the tills quicker. After a while the manager asked me to go in to the office, which was a bit of an honour really because Saturday girls didn't go and work in the office . . . I was there counting all the money from the tills, so it was a bit overwhelming with all that money. I had never seen so much in all my life.

By the 1970s, design and choice as well as function was becoming more important to shoppers and, although Woolworths survived the rise of Habitat, Next, Wilko and the growth of large supermarkets, it began to sell off its larger stores. At the time of its collapse it still had eight hundred shops in the UK. In Malvern, Woolworths closed its store on 6 January 2009. The *Malvern Gazette* of 12 January reported that Iceland had bought fifty-one former Woolworth stores, mostly in the south of England. Offering a free store to door delivery service, Iceland, a company founded in 1970 to meet the growing demand from the rising number of freezer owners, said,

> We are confident we can help support the local community in these towns.

The Supermarkets

There seems to have been a price war, or at least strong competition between the two main supermarkets in Malvern especially around the time of Dowty's photographs. Posters shown in the windows and adverts in the *Gazette* show price cuts and suggest that shoppers were being urged to spend with the promise of low prices or the attraction of Green Shield stamps (*see below*). In addition, late night shopping and an increase in the range of frozen foods on offer were promoted. The supermarkets in Malvern in 1971 were small compared to those of today but they offered a wide range of products, especially food, which might include own brands as well as those well established. The two major players in Great Malvern were Lipton's and International. There was also a Co-op and other smaller shops. So plenty of choice was available.

FINE FARE

At the top of Church Street beneath the Bluebird Café you can just see in the photograph Fine Fare shop premises closed and for sale. The

(*Opposite page*) illus. 10. Elt's and another postman (D013)

company had a long history in the UK. Its Canadian founder, a baker, moved to England in 1935 where he grew his business to become Allied Bakers (owning Fortnum and Masons and Ryvita). After a slowish start, Fine Fare from 1961 opened 130 shops and as part of Associated British Foods became the largest supermarket chain in Britain. It was sold in the 80s and became part of the Dee Corporation which owned Somerfield, later Gateway. Fine Fare's position at the top of Church Street, near to a bank and opposite the Post Office would seem to have been a good one, although there was a steep hill to get there. The premises were taken over by Robin Elt shoes who had several shops in Worcestershire, including the one next door at Orléans House. Today Elt's have their shop in the former Fine Fare location.

LIPTON'S 33–35, CHURCH STREET

Lipton's supermarket was where Boots was (closed in March 2023) and, like Fine Fare, it had a North American connection. Fifteen-year-old Thomas Lipton went from his native Glasgow to New York where he became a grocer's shop assistant and learned American marketing and sales techniques. On return to Glasgow he took over his parents' small grocery business where he put his ideas into practice. The shop was brightly lit and items displayed attractively. He was said to have worked eighteen hours a day, often sleeping on the premises. He opened more shops, founded Lipton's Tea and spread the business south into England.

BARCLAYS
BLUE BIRD
TEA ROOMS
Elt's
ELT
ORLEANS HOUSE
SHOP
FOR SALE
ELECTRICITY

Liptons
PURCHASE TAX CUTS NOW!
DEWHURST
SHERWOODS
WOOLS and
FASHIONS
QUARRY CLEANERS
119 JUY

(*Opposite page*) illus. 11. Lipton's late shopping (D155)

The Malvern shop opened in January 1971 with a full-page advert in the *Malvern Gazette* of 2 January (p.11) under the headline: 'Now open. Your new Lipton Supermarket.'

A map was provided in the advert showing the location of the supermarket and potential shoppers were told that it was close to the bus terminus and that there was car parking nearby. The pre-decimal advert featured various items available including fresh fruit, veg and meat and frozen foods and familiar brands as well as its own brand (Sunshine tinned foods). Twenty Embassy filter cigarettes cost 5/-, with Player's filter No. 6 which was becoming the new popular brand for 3/11. On the opposite page was an advertising feature (Supermarket with Sunshine touch) with information about the company (1,800 stores), the shop (on the site of a previous Maypole), and a brief biography of the manager, a local man, and his experience in retail and his involvement in various Malvern organisations. He was photographed with his assistant manager standing next to the latest large freezer. New customers got a free carrier bag in the first three weeks. Michael Dowty's July 1971 photo shows the comparatively new building with big plate glass windows. A large poster advertised late night shopping, still not a common practice but especially useful to families whose work meant that shopping during the daytime during the week was difficult. A further large advertisement in July (a couple of weeks after a huge promotional advert from International) under the Lipton's name declared:

Where fresh food is guaranteed

Save money not Stamps.

(*Opposite page*) illus. 12. International Stores purchase tax cuts (D028)

Lipton's Tea became part of Unilever in the early seventies. The *Guardian* (20/11/2021) reported that Unilever was selling its famous black tea brands because of a decline in tea sales, supermarkets reporting coffee sales almost double those of tea, and the rise in popularity of herbal and fruit infusions.

INTERNATIONAL

The main competition for Lipton's was from International. Their supermarkets were located in Church Street and in Barnard's Green. Their shop windows displayed posters with offers on prices, purchase tax cuts, and to encourage the collection of Green Shield Stamps. The *Gazette* on 15 April had an advert telling shoppers:

> From Tuesday 20 April International are giving Green Shield Stamps Double . . . until 15 May.

One of the photos of the Barnards Green branch shows a neat row of trolleys in front of the window, a young child minding a baby in a pram and gives the impression that this really was a good place to do the family shop. International put large adverts in the *Gazette* promoting offers often

OPERATIVE
Health & Speciality Foods.
INTERNATIONAL STORES
we give
GREEN SHIELD
stamps
IMMEDIATE PURCHASE TAX CUTS
GROCERIES, TOILETRIES, HOUSEWARES
MORE TO COME
GREEN SHIELD
stamps
OPEN UNTIL 8.00 EVERY FRIDAY
HAM
GREEN SHIELD
RIDGWAYS COUNTRY HOUSE
TEA
7½p
KLEENEX
KITCHEN TOWELS
16p
GREEN SHIELD
stamps
INTERNATIONAL STORES
INTERNATIONAL STORES

around the same time as Lipton's. Examples of 1971 prices include PG Tips 7 1/2p a quarter, Jacob's Cream Crackers 5p a pack, Golden Shred Marmalade 1lb jar for 9 1/2p. International Church Street branch stood where Church Walk starts now. The 1981 Goad's plan records that it was demolished for access to the area, the former builder's yards off Edith Walk, and that a new International supermarket was to be built there with its bakery, butchers, fresh fish counters and a crèche where children could be left while adults shopped. It soon became Somerfield's and later for a short time a Co-op and eventually Wilkinson's, now Wilko.

An old photograph in Brian Iles's collection shows that the Church Street site had once been the premises of one of Malvern's early garages, W. H. Mayo, with everything for the motorist, including motor spirit (petrol).

CO-OP SUPERMARKET, 61–63 CHURCH STREET

Most high streets at one time had a Co-op shop. The frontage of the one in the Malvern photograph is deceptive. (*See illus. 12, D028.*) Goad's plan shows that the premises were much larger than the frontage suggests. The Co-operative movement started in 1844 in Rochdale with members contributing capital to be able to start trading a small range of essential food and goods. It expanded rapidly during the nineteenth century. The Co-op used to have a dividend scheme for members which allowed them to build up savings to purchase goods. It went on to give stamps which were the Co-op blue colour. There is no longer a Co-op in Church Street but branches continue nearby in Malvern Link and Barnards Green. By 1990, the Church Street premises became a Freeman Hardy and Willis shoe shop. It is now Caffe Nero.

THE RETAIL PARK

The retail park of the 1990s is on the edge of the built-up area of Malvern. The shopping centre has a large car park adjacent to shop premises with well-known names (e.g. Morrisons, Marks and Spencer, Boots) and a MacDonalds. There is also access by bus. It has created a shift in the shopping habits of many people.

In Great Malvern itself, Iceland continues to thrive and give a service at competitive prices, especially on frozen foods, from the previous Woolworth site in Church Street.

Waitrose came to Malvern in 1999 following huge earth moving and levelling operations to create the site for the shop. The design included an extensive car park for those who lived outside the centre of Great Malvern or who liked or needed to do a big weekly shop. For many it is within walking distance. It's range of food and other goods and services and its staff-partners (it is part of the John Lewis Partnership) live up to its existing reputation for quality.

At the time of writing, Aldi (originally a German supermarket) has recently opened a large store just beyond the retail park. It has a reputation for good value. It will be interesting to see the effect it has on shopping habits in Malvern.

(*Opposite page*) illus. 13. The Retail Park (RS)

Green Shield Stamps

The concept of shops issuing stamps which were collected by shoppers and stuck into books, to be redeemed later for household goods chosen from a catalogue began in the United States in the late nineteenth century. In the UK Green Shield Stamps became a registered trade mark in the 1950s. By the 70s stamps were used as incentives in the competitive markets of garage and supermarket sales as in the case of International and Lipton's outlined above. The chairman of the company was reported to be the highest paid executive in the country. He was entitled to £395,000 but waived £135,000 of his pay. Over time, however, the novelty of Green Shield Stamps began to wear off. Some considered it tedious to stick in all the stamps being offered and the value of the goods as rewards was in decline. Customers for a while were allowed to top up stamps with cash for more valuable rewards. Eventually the system gave rise to Argos later in the 1970s and stamps went out of use in the eighties. Today on-line shopping and the rise of Amazon continues to change the face of all kinds of traditional shopping methods and incentives. Argos is now owned by Sainsbury's. A few outlets have recently closed.

McDonald's
Malvern shopping park
Malvern shopping park
M&S
MATALAN
MOUNTAIN WAREHOUSE
Specsavers
next
pets at home
Boots
NEW LOOK
Argos
shoezone
£ pound stretcher
TOOLSTATION
OPEN TO ALL 7 DAYS A WEEK
Poundland
CAFFE NERO
halfords
Card Factory
COSTA
Superdrug
CUSHMAN & WAKEFIELD
Helpdesk
0845 6031485

Butchers

CRIDLAN AND WALKERS

The shop is now Mac and Jac's cafe in its stunning Gothic style building (Grade II listed) dating back to 1830. The 1971 photo shows it as Cridlan and Walker's butchers shop which sold a range of high-class meats and fruit and vegetables. The name of Cridlan can still be seen on the outside etched on the stone facing under the windows and the interior of the front of the café has retained the butcher's practical black and white tiled floors.

DEWHURST'S, 37 CHURCH STREET

This butcher next door to Lipton's in 1971 was one of a chain of butchers' shops founded by the Vestey family from their shop in Liverpool in 1897. In the last century it had at one time 1,400 outlets so was a common sight in most high streets and a trusted supplier to many families. It went into administration in 2006. The *Guardian* (20/07/2011) reported research which placed Dewhurst as the third most missed retailer among those that have closed in the last ten years. The brand was acquired by Brand Cellar who buy up dormant names. In Malvern, Malvern Country Meats traded from the premises which later became Lace, and more recently Reclaimers, selling vintage clothes. It is now an attractive shop selling children's shoes called To Boot.

(*Top*) illus. 15. Original sign (JC82)

(*Right*) illus. 14. Cridlan and Walkers (D078)

BAXTER'S, 20 WORCESTER ROAD

In 1960s this shop was the London Central Meat Company which had a number of butcher's shops around the country including in Leamington Spa. It had its origins in Tamworth market in Staffordshire. It changed to Baxter's in the late 1950s and this is the name on the 1971 Goad's Plan. By the 1980s the premises were occupied by the Red Windmill Unisex Boutique and later David Kellsall, followed by Taylors who had an estate agent's business here and in the neighbouring former Parcel's Office at number 18. It was until recently the Terrace-on-the-Hill restaurant.

(*Opposite page*) illus. 16. End of morning sweep Church Street (D039)

NEWMAN'S, MALVERN LINK

An article in the *Gazette* had the headline (17/6/71 p 13): 'Deep freezers can warm the hearts of busy housewives.'

Freezers were among the most desirable household items in the early seventies. Although most refrigerators had small ice boxes, they did not have enough space for the variety and quantity of frozen food becoming available or to allow for fresh food to be frozen.

Jane Shawyer commented,

> Newman's the butchers. They were in the Link where Domino's Pizza is now. And I can remember they sold freezers which was a new commodity at the time.

SHERWOODS
WOOLS and
FASHIONS
DEWHURST
SALE
38 CAB

FREEZER
FOR BEST QUALITY
R. Newman.
ENGLISH MEAT
DEEP FREEZER FOOD SUPPLIES
No 122
ON SALE HERE
Walls
ICE CREAM

(*Opposite page*) illus. 17. R. Newman Malvern Link (D114)

(*Below*) illus. 18. Newman's advert

SAVE SAVE SAVE

Come and See for Yourself the Finest Selection of FROZEN FOODS at

R. NEWMAN

BUTCHERS

CASH AND CARRY

DEEP FREEZE CENTRE

With a freezer, you can save up to 20% on food bills. On bulk-priced meat, catering packs of frozen food, fruit and vegetables. And you have the convenience of a choice of food always on hand.

A SELECTION FROM OUR PRICE LIST

All Meat packed to your requirements

20lb. English Top Side	42p per lb.
20lb. Rolled Rib English	35p per lb.
½ New Zealand Lamb	17½p per lb.
2 Leg Pork, English	23p per lb.
10lb. Pork Chops	30p per lb.
10lb. N.Z. Lamb Cutlets	19p per lb.
20lb. Peas	7½p per lb.
6 Chicken	16p per lb.

Let us supply you with a

DEEP FREEZER

to take advantage of these prices

HELIFROST 12, 16 and 17 cu. ft.

McKENZIE 12 cu. ft.

And now in stock the popular BEEKAY 16 cu. ft.

PRICES FROM £67

H.P. TERMS AVAILABLE

Only £10 Deposit on any model

And Marcella Hales said,

> I remember when freezers came out. There was a huge excitement when you could actually freeze food.

Roy Harris remembered the days before freezers were a common item:

> I do recall my mother having a freezer probably as early as the mid '60s but then we had a fridge in the late '50s. It was a large chest freezer which took up a significant amount of room in a relatively small kitchen but by that stage the coal fired oven had been removed to create some space. I can certainly remember it being used to store fruit and vegetables picked during season and then used out of season, unlike today when everything seems to be always in season – no longer a treat to have runner beans in August. We probably also used it to buy some bulk meat. The forerunner to the freezer in our house was a home canning machine which was used to seal blank tin cans from the Metal Box in Worcester. Basically you roll sealed a lid to the can and then cooked the can in water to preserve the contents.

SLATER'S, LINK TOP

The photograph shows how traditional greengrocers also stocked frozen foods. Findus frozen foods are advertised on the window so the shop no longer had to rely on seasonal fresh vegetables and fruit, although these are set out enticingly in traditional boxes on the pavement with prices clearly displayed. This photo also shows that people were quite happy to leave a pushchair and a bicycle unattended outside while they shopped.

(*Opposite page*) illus. 19. Slater's greengrocers (D103)

Grocers

MALVERN MINI MARKET4 BELLE VUE TERRACE

On the Goad 1971 plan there is a grocery shop on the Terrace in the row now occupied by Ask Italian. The name suggests perhaps it was the equivalent of what we would today call a convenience shop. (*See illus. 62, M.E.B., D009, p.116.*)

Home Deliveries and Stockers

Jane Shawyer remembers from her childhood the days before supermarkets:

> I remember my mother getting her groceries from, before the supermarkets came into being, from Stocker's. I think the shop was called Stocker's . . . It was quite sensible then in those days because my mum had regular items that she had delivered each week, a quarter of tea or whatever the things were. Every single week. They knew that she wanted these things, and they would deliver these every week without her phoning up. If she wanted something extra, she would just phone up and add those things to the order and of course they would deliver on a certain day of the week.

GREENGROCER & FRUITERER
FINDUS
FINDUS
ENGLISH CHERRIES 10P lb!
ENGLISH CHERRIES
GREENGROCER & FRUITERER

And my mother didn't drive, and it was amazing at that time because you could have all sorts of things delivered. We had Mr Brickell, the baker – he would deliver the bread. We had a man who delivered eggs – we didn't know his name – we called him Eggy (I don't think he ever knew that). And we had a gentleman, again I can't remember his name, but he came round in a blue van delivering fruit and vegetables. My mum would leave a bag outside the door with [a list of] what items she wanted from the van. He would fill up the bag and bring it to the door for her. So, it was all very sensible. She didn't have to go and carry bags all round from the shops.

(*Opposite page*) illus. 20. Church Street from Priory Grounds (D027). See also illus. 21.

Delicatessen

RAINFORD SHARPE'S, 77–79 CHURCH STREET

In 1971 it was Rainford Sharpe's delicatessen and grocery shop which occupied these premises at 77 Church Street. Karen Hill described the interior of the shop her mother used to visit on Friday mornings when in town shopping with friends:

> It was a local delicatessen where you went down a stair in to the shop. It always seemed rather dark. The ceiling was very low. It had glass counters which the staff served from behind and the meats and cheese and fish were all laid out. And on the other side it had staff serving from a counter with packets and tinned goods.

GEORGE'S dry
Sharpe
PETTIFORS

Until the 1960s, Rainford Sharpe's also had a shop in Barnard's Green. Although people remembered staff serving from counters as in the above account, its advert proclaimed that the shops are:

> Malvern's most modern self-selection food stores.

The Bespoke Hair Company is in the Church Street premises now. In the 1990s it had been Lunn Poly Travel Agents. Holidays abroad started to become popular in the late sixties.

Bakers

BARLOW'S, 57 CHURCH STREET

Barlow's bakers were at 57 Church Street in the seventies where Malvern Nails and Spa is now. From the 1980s, it was a fresh fruit and vegetable shop. (*See also illus. 33, p.74.*)

The photo with the three differently named bread delivery vans parked in a row in Church Street suggests that most people bought their bread in one of the nearby supermarkets, the probable destination of the contents from the bread vans.

The vans represented three of the big brands available in the UK and at the time were owned by the giants of the baking industry. Wonderloaf had its origins in the USA which produced one of the first white sliced loaves

(*Opposite page*) illus. 21.
Three of a kind bread delivery (D041)

derloaf
ARF 352D
TXC 632F
Sunblest
baked by PALMER'S locally
Rainford Sharpe
Real bread but lighter
Mothers Pri
BREAD

in the 1930s. It had 80 per cent of the US market and gave rise the saying 'the best thing since sliced bread'. After the Second World War, in the '50s sliced wrapped loaves were reintroduced. Improvements in production and the rise of the supermarkets coupled with simple convenience encouraged the market to grow. In the UK Sunblest, founded in the 1940s, belonged to Allied Bakeries. Mothers Pride was a sub-brand of Hovis originally made in Glasgow and later produced by British Bakers. Mothers Pride was the UK's best-selling brand in the 1970s and 80s. Today while most people probably buy bread from supermarkets, there are still bakers' shops in the Malvern area including local bakers, Colston, and the family firm based in Bristol, Parsons. With a recent interest in artisan bakeries producing specialist breads, the Malvern Bakehouse is a recent addition for shoppers in Church Street.

(*Opposite page*) illus. 22. Morning milk (D034)

Milk

The photographs show bottles of milk standing outside a couple of premises in the town centre. There was a dairy, Cutler's Dairy, at Malvern Link. In the seventies milk could still be delivered to the door, usually daily except Sundays. The milk was usually sold as pasteurised or sterilised and came in glass bottles which were put out when empty for the dairy to collect, clean and re-use. Today we can buy different kinds of milk in cartons, including long-life, and non-dairy alternatives from supermarkets, convenience stores and farm shops and other outlets. On-line ordering

DO IT YOURSELF
KITS
BLACK & DECKER
BRIDGES
REVO
WOLF

enables some producers, for example Bennett's Farms, to do doorstep deliveries today, often combining milk with groceries. School children used to be given free school milk but this came to an end for the seven- to eleven-year-olds in 1971 earning the then Education Minister the title in some of the newspapers 'The milk snatcher.'

Confectioners, Cafés and Restaurants

THE BLUEBIRD TEA ROOMS (ABOVE THE FORMER FINE FARE)

The Bluebird Tea Rooms above Elt's were started in 1913 by a Miss Hunt. Some of the furniture still in use is original, possibly older than the tea room itself. Composer Edward Elgar and the architect Troyte Griffiths used to visit for their morning coffee. Today the Bluebird is still there. As well as traditional scones and cakes, there is a selection of freshly prepared food with special dietary needs well catered for. In the early 1970s, dietary needs were not always recognised and not necessarily catered for by small cafés and restaurants. Dietary supplements became more readily available and health food shops were beginning to appear. In Malvern there was an example, the Health Food Store, at number 65 Church Street. The novelist Barbara Cartland, who was from Malvern, was an enthusiastic supporter of supplements and healthy eating and endorsed one supplement in *Malvern Gazette* adverts. Barbara Cartland's *Health Food Cookery Book* was published in paperback in 1971.

Illus. 23. Bluebird Tea Rooms sign (Image courtesy of Caroline Burton, the Bluebird Tea Rooms).

(*Opposite page*) illus. 24. Dorothy Café (D095).

SPORTS DEPOT LTD
VACUUM SALES & SERVICE
The DOROTHY CAFÉ
SPORTS DEPOT

THE DOROTHY CAFÉ, 10 CHURCH STREET

The café in the photo stands in a row which at the time began with the Fermor Arms and ended with the Sports Depot. It was a favourite high-class cake shop and café for visitors and shoppers. David Burley referred to it as,

> Owned and run by Miss Schneider (a Swiss lady) who named it after her best friend. As well as the restaurant, they had a magnificent display of cakes from Brunner's of Cheltenham.

Karen Hill described her visits:

> The Women's Institute held a Friday produce market in the Lyttleton Well Building were my mother and her friends shopped each week . . . I remember well the Dorothy Café with its extensive range of cakes which you could buy to eat in the café or to take home. I was allowed to choose from this long glass counter a cake to have with a drink of milk.

THE PROMENADE RESTAURANT, 41 WORCESTER ROAD

The restaurant was here for many years. Its recently renovated premises are currently Detour, a shop specialising in everything for the cyclist. An antiques shop, Promenade Antiques, was here before. Carlton Antiques occupied number 43, then Foley Antiques, now the florists, Blackbird.

On the window of Detour, just visible, is the name of a former occupant George Smith's the Bakers. He had also run the restaurant. In the seventies the Restaurant was popular with visitors from Birmingham who often came in coachloads. June Tilt described the restaurant she used to run with her husband.

> The restaurant was in a row of shops two doors away from Brays. So you went straight in off the pavement through the door into the restaurant proper. And I had two waitresses to look after the customers and my husband was in the kitchen doing all the cooking. It was very old-fashioned tables with four chairs . . . There was a 'dumb waiter' – a rather large wooden contraption – which you don't see very often these days. The order would be sent down with a written order for lunch. Then we'd plate it all up and ring the bell and send the 'dumb waiter' up to the top . . . I looked very serious dressed up all in a black skirt, white blouse and a frilly pinner.
>
> By 1972 we had different coins, different denominations. There was lots of information on the wireless and television news, lots of pictures of the coins telling you anything they needed you to know. But it was going to happen, and nobody could say no . . . We were very busy on a Saturday and Sunday. We had a coach that came. Regularly brought a coach load of people. There was a second restaurant above the ground floor and that was laid out and the people went straight up and had a set tea.

Jane Tinklin, June's daughter, added,

> The dumb waiter – I can remember my sister getting in to that and going down in it!

Jane also said,

> The flat upstairs was on two floors and had a skylight above the stairs . . . There was a back entrance to the accommodation from Queens Drive with a metal bridge and steps over the alley which ran the full length of the rear of the Bray's building.

REBECCA'S RESTAURANT, 36 BELLE VIEW TERRACE

This restaurant had belonged to Warwick House and was adjacent to the Man's Shop. It later became a bar and bistro and was part of the popular Gallery 36 which closed in September 2022, the *Gazette* quoting the increased cost in utilities bills as the reason. The premises have recently (March 2023) been sold.

TAI WO RESTAURANT, 5 WORCESTER ROAD

The restaurant was here in 1971 in premises occupied previously by the Worcester Co-op. It continued throughout the eighties and nineties and became the Bengal Brasserie Indian restaurant in the early twenty-first century. The premises are now known as the Yak and Yeti.

Illus. 25. Mosaic (JC79)

MORLEY'S, 12 BELLE VUE TERRACE

This small shop next door to W. H. Smith has a very attractive frontage. In 1971 when Michael Dowty took his photograph it was Morley's Confectioners with the name of the owner inscribed on the mosaic threshold.

One customer has described it as

> having mirrors on the walls and shelves on which stood glass jars full of different kinds of sweets for customers to select from, including little sugar roses and violets.

It was a traditional kind of sweet shop, perhaps reflecting the age of the company. The window display shows that it also sold cigarettes. The Morleys were originally from the south of England and Henry Morley and his brothers and sisters lived for some time in London. Henry in the 1890s was a grocer's clerk. He later moved to Worcester where he married Louisa Price. By the 1910s Henry had shops in Cheltenham and, trading as L. Morley purveyor of high-class confectionery, had two shops in Birmingham, three in Worcester and a branch here at Belle Vue Terrace, Malvern. In Worcester he was attracted to an employee, a young local woman, Kate Philips. Abandoning his wife and daughter (and, it was alleged, taking funds to start a new business in the United States), he booked two second class tickets for Kate and himself as Mr and Mrs

L. MORLEY
Wall's
& SON
HIGH CLASS
CONFECTIONERY
CASTELLA
REGAL
STOL
VIRGINIA
No 10
W & J. BURROW Ltd
MALVERN WATER
(ENTRANCE)

(*Opposite page*) illus. 26. Newspaper bundles (D010)

Marshall. The ship for their voyage was the *Titanic*. Henry was lost in the disaster but Kate survived and returned to Worcester.

The shop is now the One Nail Bar.

Clothes and Fashion

Rose Arno talking about her wedding reception said,

> The head waiter was in charge of proceedings and wasn't keen to let our best man in because he had long hair and a suit that didn't match!

Roy Harris said,

> I recall fashion jeans becoming popular in my mid-teens and being very disappointed when my mother tried to impress me by buying me a pair of blue jeans from the Co-op – they were work jeans.

Gill Holt recalled,

> I had a long skirt. I made all our clothes. There was no easy way of buying cheap clothes – homemade clothes, no mobile phones, no computers . . .

KAYS CATALOGUE

Kays of Worcester were one of the most successful mail order companies in the country. It enabled people to pay by instalments and its well-illustrated catalogues influenced the way many people dressed. Mary Quant (designer of the mini skirt and hot pants) designed for the catalogue in the sixties. At the end of that decade Kays were sending out around 80,000 catalogues a day. Its extensive archive was based at Worcester University but a new home for the archive is currently being sought (MG 17/03/2023).

Sally Trepte (Warwick House) and Christopher Davis (Brays) both noted the move towards more casual clothes for everyday wear.

Clothes were becoming classless, informal and unisex and one of the increasingly common trends was for blue denim jeans which spread from the US workwear to almost universal wear for young men and women and, as time went on, for almost all of us. The 1971 photos indicate that the kinds of clothes worn often depended on the age of the wearer as well as personal preference.

(*Opposite page*) illus. 27. Abbey House Bus Stop (D079)

ABBEY LINEN AND CHILDREN'S WEAR

The photograph shows that these premises were then a largish shop selling a wide range of children's clothes. Local people may remember the shop as MacFisheries, a chain of fresh fish shops in the twentieth century. It had been a fish shop selling Severn salmon for many years

Abbey House
BABY LINEN
CHILDRENS
WEAR SPECIALISTS
HALIFAX

before. Now First Paige's printers operate a design and print and photocopying service here. They also publish and sell a wide selection of local interest books, cards and calendars. They have another shop in Worcester.

NESTA CHILDREN'S WEAR AND GOODS, 39 WORCESTER ROAD

The Promenade building following along from Brays was built in red brick in, according to the plaque at the top of it, in 1891. In the 1960s the first shop along from Brays was known as Nesta Baby Furniture and Toys with a slight change of name appearing on Goad's plan of 1971. It later became a gift shop. Soundwaves electronics business operated from here in the nineties and first part of the current century selling consumer electronics and giving advice on use and maintenance. The Promenade building is being renovated at the time of writing and new businesses are occupying the shops. There are apartments above.

LEATHER AND FAYRE

This shop at 111–113 Church Street round the corner from Burston's sold a selection of leather goods, as its name suggests, and was also a popular toy shop. Toys were often also sold in shops selling children's clothes. It is now the Bay Leaf restaurant with its Indian cuisine.

SHERWOOD'S, 39 CHURCH STREET

(*See illus. 16. End of morning sweep above with Dewhurst's, Church Street, D039, p.41.*)

Sherwood's small shop in Church Street sold knitting wools and ladies fashions, their window in the photograph showing, mostly, separates. Like many other traders they held sales in the summer. Malvern Barbers now have the shop which is busy producing today's fashionable hairdressing for men and boys. On the mosaic threshold at the entrance you can just make out the remains of the name of Norman May, the well-known Malvern photographer who at one time operated from here. He also wrote guide books – copies can be found in Malvern Library reference section. In the rear of these premises, original stained-glass windows have survived.

WERFF'S, 85–87 CHURCH STREET

(*See illus. 20 and 55. Parking in Church Street, D043.*)

Werff's of Bond Street had shops in several towns including Worcester. In Malvern in the seventies the shop was in the current Parsons bakery premises. It sold a range of ladies' fashions and has been described by one satisfied customer as

> a nice little shop.

It was still trading there in 1981. A photograph of the Worcester shop interior and a personal advert selling a jacket from Werff's shows that the shop displayed and sold well-made, rather smart and fashionable clothes.

MARIE, 27 CHURCH STREET

One of the long-lasting businesses near the top of Church Street was known in 1971 as Marie-lingerie. The advertisements in the *Malvern Gazette* inform us that they were stockists for Berlei , an international brand and well-known company in the UK , originally founded in Australia by a Mr Burley who changed the spelling to look more enticingly French! The corsetiere was in Church Street in the late fifties and sixties, launched by Marie Huddleston and Nora James in 1959. It was taken over when they retired by David and Pat Egerton. The shop continued as Marie-lingerie into the nineties. The business doubtless had a loyal clientele. Christopher Davis takes up the story about Marie's.

> Pat had earlier been a member of Brays staff . . . In 1989 David died suddenly and Pat approached me with a view to combining her business with ours. In February 1990 Pat returned to the Bray's staff . . . Marie's merchandise augmented and to a large extent complemented the existing Bray's stock and the merger proved beneficial to all concerned.

The adverts for Berlei sales in the summer at Warwick House and

Brays in the *Gazette* have the headline: 'It's the Berlei fit that sets you free.'

It goes on to say that this means you can decide on a whether you need a girdle with Medium or Firm Control and says that they all have 'tummy'-flattening panels. The then comparatively recent invention of Lycra as a textile with elastic properties began to change the production of underwear so that it became more simplified and, together with tights, meant that by the mid-seventies underwear for many women was unstructured and minimal. Although the drawings in the 1971 adverts are of young women, in reality the products would be likely to be sold to an older market. Young women would be unlikely to want anything to hold stockings up – they would be bare legged in the summer or wear tights at other times and would find such underwear restricting.

Hairdressers

BURLEY'S, 8 WORCESTER ROAD

The family firm of Burleys had their premises on the Worcester Road in part of the former Bath and Pump Room premises (built in 1822 for the water cure visitors), next door in 1971 to Martin's Opticians and to what until recently was Barclays Bank. In 1970 Burley's celebrated fifty years of caring for the hair of visitors and residents. They also had contracts with some of the public schools. During the Shaw Festival season at the theatre, George Bernard Shaw not only premièred his play *The Apple*

Cart but also had his beard trimmed by Burley's. Arthur Conan Doyle, creator of Sherlock Holmes was another famous client. At one time six generations of the family worked at the shop where Harry Burley had started the business in 1920. When it closed a few years ago, some of the fittings, for example 1920s mirrors and 1960s Formica work tops, were still in place. A Museum of Hairdressing in Leicester agreed to take many of the contents including the entire contents of the upstairs salon and the pink neon sign from the front according to the *Worcester News* (30/8/2019). The premises are currently for sale and are used as a base for an antiques and bygones business.

(*Opposite page*) illus. 28. Burley's and Barclays Bank (D101)

ABBEY STYLISTS, 3 ABBEY ROAD

The ladies' hairdresser occupied the shop which is now Hunky Dorey with its attractively displayed pre-loved items. It had been a hairdressers in the sixties and is on plans under this name into the nineties after which it became a small art gallery.

SHELLEY'S, 1 EDITH WALK

There was a ladies' hairdresser's at the top of Edith Walk in 1971. Ten years later it was Pic-Nic Basket Restaurant, later Truly Scrumptious Café. In more recent years there was a hairdressers upstairs. Currently the premises are occupied by Rise Plant Kitchen + Movement Studio, an imaginative approach to well-being.

BURLEY'S
BARCLAYS BAN
REDDINGS TEA

VICTOR'S COIFFEUR

Victor's was located in Warwick House which sublet it to the hairdressing business. Sally Trepte describes it in the sixties in her book when a weekly shampoo and set was a routine for some women. For many it would have continued into the 70s. Hair was washed and put on to rollers and the client would sit under a hood dryer, was usually provided with a women's fashion magazine, until ready for the rest of the hairdresser's art. The fashion for women's hair to be coloured a non-traditional hair colour is comparatively recent. Today women and men have far greater choice of styles and products than in the seventies. Turkish barbers are now a popular option for men's hairdressing.

Haircuts

Longer hair for young men can be seen on several of the photographs. It was not always acceptable to some of the older generation.

Gill Holt said:

> My son had long hair in the 1970s. He was at Hanley Castle Grammar School. I was called in to see the headmaster about him. He had given him the money to go and have his hair cut.

Makeup and Cosmetics

In the seventies, there were several trends ranging from a natural look to a super sheen but on the whole the look tended to be subtle. Revlon and Mary Quant were popular brands and Yardley's Tweed perfume was still used by many. Women often tended to choose what suited them rather than be slaves to fashion.

Tattoos were still the province of merchant seamen and the navy. Although tattoos have a very long history, they were in the nineteenth century only appearing on women in the circuses and fairgrounds mostly in the US. The trend for both men and women to body art is a fairly recent one and has migrated to fashion from reflecting allegiance to a particular group (e.g. Hell's Angels). Great Malvern's studio, Lumina, has opened within the last few years. There are some interesting photographs of nineteenth-century tattooed women just inside its entrance door.

Drycleaners

QUALITY DRY CLEANERS, 47–51 CHURCH STREET

The TSB has fairly recently vacated the premises at 47-51 Church Street where in 1971 Quality Dry cleaners advertised hot pants cleaning costed by the inch! Mary Quant is credited with the introduction of hot pants to fashion in the mid-sixties. Made in many different fabrics,

QUALITY CLEANERS
4 HOUR CLEANING
No extra charge
Saturdays included
for most articles
hot pants
3p OFF
EFK 881C

(*Above*) illus. 30. Hot pants (D156)

(*Opposite page*) illus. 29.
Quality Cleaners & bike (D082)

hot pants could be bought for around £2 and were popular with young women. It was reported in the press that parents often objected – 'You're not going out in those'!

It was not uncommon for people to have knitwear dry cleaned, which otherwise would usually require, if wool, careful washing by hand in Lux or Dreft, rolling in a towel to take away some of the water and then drying flat. Quality Dry Cleaners, known as Priory Dry Cleaners in the 1990s, had previously had premises at number 22 Church Street (where Oxfam is today) next to the Oxley's Music Shop.

ST GEORGE'S DRY CLEANERS, 73–75 CHURCH STREET

Another dry cleaner's shop was in Church Street, indicating the demand for this service, especially for large items (curtains, for example) or for fabrics or special outfits needing treatments beyond ordinary washing.

Washing machines in the seventies did not have the range of programmes available to us today and some items could also be a problem to dry quickly. The first washing machines which could wash and dry in the same drum were not always reliable and it was not until the late seventies with better mechanics and microtechnology that reliability and performance improved and made them suited to the domestic market. They became the automatics we use today.

Malvern Pharmacy (Murray's, now part of the Peak Pharmacy Group) now occupies the premises.

Shoes and Shoe Repairs

ELT'S FOOTWEAR, 15–17 CHURCH STREET

Where Elt's is now, in the 1971 photo had been a Fine Fare supermarket displaying a 'for sale' notice. Elt's shop was next door in Orleans House. They bought the former Fine Fare premises and extended the business. Their shop had a children's department with a little roundabout for children to use while waiting to have their shoes fitted.

The x-ray machine (quite common equipment in shoe shops) was advertised as 'perfectly harmless for children'. There had been a women's shoe department with quite glamorous decorative furnishings and a men's department with hunting scenes on the walls. Orleans House is now Dynastic Art, a shop selling accessories and a selection of women's wear including Italian jumpers. In recent years the shop here sold outdoor clothing and walking boots under the name of Time Outdoors and, later, Elements. The windows above have some nice original glass. As Orleans House, in earlier times, it had been Thirlwall and Thorntons Drapers. Elt's is a family business with other shops in the county including in Worcester. In 2022 it celebrated its 150th anniversary.

Other shoe shops in 1971 in Church Street included Lennard's at 93–95 where the YMCA Charity Shop is now. It has a long history. It joined Benefit Footwear Ltd and later became part of the British Shoe Corporation. Freeman Hardy and Willis continued at number 59 into

(*Above*) illus. 31. Roundabout (JC – image courtesy of Elt's Archive)

(*Opposite page*) illus. 32. Top of Church Street (D195)

BARCLAYS
Elt's
ELTS
ORLEANS HOUSE
Clarks
SHOES
BLUE BIRD
TEA ROOMS
SHOP
FOR SALE

the 1980s. This company also had a long history, the brand going back to 1879 with its origins in Leicester. It too became part of the British Shoe Corporation. The Shaw Trust charity has its shop there now.

(*Above*) illus. 33. Freeman Hardy and Willis (D042)

(*Opposite page*) illus. 34. C. Lowe shoe repairs (D137)

C. LOWE

In the photograph of 1971 there is at the rear of Church Street an image of the premises of C. Lowe, footwear repairs. The name was used into the 1990s. It has only recently closed and will be missed by many. Lowe's also recycled leather goods. The shop could be accessed via the back of the Great Malvern Hotel and Wilko. There was also an entrance next to the Fig restaurant via the archway. This may originally have been access to stabling for the Belle Vue Hotel as shown on a map of 1842. There is evidence of old brickwork and boarding, perhaps a hayloft.

BRIDGEWATER FOOTWEAR REPAIR, 18 BELLE VUE TERRACE

Bridgewater and Son were listed as bootmakers in earlier directories but by 1971 called themselves footwear repairers. The premises later became Tizzies ladies wear and is now the Turkish Barbers.

C. LOWE.
SHOE REPAIRS

I. PARRY
JEWELLER
WATCHMAKER
INGERSOLL

(*Opposite page*) illus. 35. Parry's, about 1969 (courtesy of Parry's/Nick Hetherington)

Jewellers

PARRY'S, 115 CHURCH STREET

Parry's the jewellers is a long-established Malvern business trading here under the same name today as it was in 1971 when it was owned by Idris and Mary Parry. The shop was taken over by David and Felicity Siviter who ran the business until 2017. It has been owned by Nick Hetherington since 2018. The present attractive windows were designed in 1997 and are much more in harmony with the building than the former rather plain ones which would have been familiar to 1971 customers. In the past the premises had been the showroom of the West Midlands Gas Board. Today, Parry's expert service is valued both for new purchases and access to repairs for old and valued jewellery. The business has recently celebrated its seventieth anniversary.

Interiors, Soft Furnishings, China, Gifts and Household Goods

GORDON SMITH'S, 53–55 CHURCH STREET

Gordon Smith's, famed today for a huge range of textiles and soft furnishings, has existed since 1935. It is a family business selling fabrics, providing a curtain making service and selling bedding and towels, with cookware and china upstairs. In its 1971 summer sales you could buy pillow cases for 25p each and sheets for £3.50 a pair. In 1891 and for many years later, Gwynn and Sons had a workshop here selling furniture. The name still appears in an advert for Gordon Smith's in 2011.[1] Gwynn's were also undertakers.

Illus. 36. Malvern Studios (photo courtesy of Les Hall and Malvern Studios)

MALVERN STUDIOS, 56 COWLEIGH ROAD

Malvern Studios is a well-known business established in the 1960s by Leslie Hall. Les used his cabinet making, carpentry and wood carving skills to build an enterprise which produced and supplied fine and antique furniture and interior furnishings to stately homes, museums as well as commissioned pieces for private clients and running a retail shop. Members of the British Antique Furniture Restorers Association, Malvern Studios are also well known for their lighting, mirrors and table lamps. In 1971 Les's son Jeff joined the family firm which in 2011 celebrated its fiftieth anniversary. The shop premises have been extended over the years. The family has played an important role in the Cowleigh Community.

CHAS E. BISHOP, 20 BELLE VUE TERRACE

Bishop's had a drapers, underwear, household linens and soft furnishings shop here in the 1960s but on the Goad's 1971 plan are described briefly

1. Gordon Smith (Malvern) Ltd, inc. Gwynn and Sons est. 1862

as 'fabrics'. In 2000 it was Malvern Curtains and Drapery and in 1971 was a neighbour of Clarke Roxborough insurance office, the company which owned the Burrows Factory site. Prezzo the Italian Restaurant has recently closed its restaurant in these premises. The Prezzo chain closed further restaurants in April 2023 blaming inflation and the rising energy costs and food prices.

PETTIFOR'S, 81–83 CHURCH STREET

(*See illus. 20, D027, with Rainford Sharps, p.47.*)

EE Get Connected is at number 81 where in 1971 Pettifor's sold a range of household goods. Their premises from Goad's plan looks as if they may have occupied the present Carnival Records shop too. Currently the entrance to Anupam Restaurant is here. Perhaps this arcade with Parsons Bakery now on the far side may have been originally a service entrance to the hotel behind it.

VACUUM SALES AND SERVICE SHOP, 10B CHURCH STREET

(*See illus.24. Dorothy Café, D095, p.53.*)

This specialist shop was located next to the Dorothy Café in the row of shops which were to be demolished and rebuilt in 1981. It was another example of a shop which enabled families to not only choose and buy equipment but have the assurance that it could be maintained in good order and repaired by the shop when necessary.

OXFAM GIFTS, 4A BELLE VUE TERRACE

(*See illus. 62. MEB, D009.*)

Oxfam Gifts is shown on Goad's plan as a tiny shop on Belle Vue Terrace, backing on to the area to the side of the Unicorn pub. Leather Crafts had the shop in 1981 and in the following decade it was Freak Bros. T-shirts Records and Comics. Was Oxfam Gifts the first charity shop in Great Malvern? The shop was vacant for some time, then became the Smokehouse Deli. Recently the shop has been Waffles, Crepes, Pancakes, Shakes.

THE CHINA SHOP, 45 WORCESTER ROAD

This shop was the last in the row of shops in the Promenade building. It sold a wide range of china and glass in the 1970s. In the 1960 directory it was listed as an antiques shop. Now renovated following many years as the Nearly New Boutique, it is Heidi's a toyshop with a range of toys, jigsaws and books for young children.

Illus. 37. Colemans, formerly Woods China and Glass (2021 Coleman 2 JC)

WOODS CHINA AND GLASS, 3–5 CHURCH STREET

Coleman's stationery shop at this address looked narrower inside than the outside suggests. The building was erected in 1877. The attractive double window frontage is very possibly original. Here at least a hundred years ago (and in 1971) was Woods China and Glass Shop.

Karen Hill remembered,

> Fine china was purchased from Woods China shop which was next to the Midland Bank at the top of Church Street.

And Jane Tinklin recalled visits as a young child,

> I remember mum telling me to keep still and put my hands in my pockets so that I didn't break anything.

In 1990 the shop was Heritage China and Glass and later became Classic Gifts. Colemans took the premises in 2004/5. Their range and knowledge of art supplies was valued by students from the College of Art and local artists. At the time of writing, the Colemans have just retired and the premises are being renovated to become a bookshop. Sarah Coleman said that above the shop there are now five apartments, some with original sash windows. Their rooms originally had ornate Victorian fireplaces. There may have been stables to the rear.

Florists

JANE'S FLOWER SHOP, 107–109 CHURCH STREET

Jane's flower shop was next to Burston's in Church Street in 1971. It has existed as a florists with a few variations in its name into the present century. The shop is now Tunics Plus with its wide selection of women's wear, especially tunics!

(*Opposite page*) illus. 38. Malvern Library (D133)

Chapter Two
The Library and the Bookshops

Malvern Library

Malvern Library in Graham Road is a popular place to visit to borrow from a wide range of books, read the papers, use local history books and the reference section, use computers to access information beyond the library itself, borrow and return library loans and consult the helpful and knowledgeable staff. The children's library provides a great selection of books and activities. Other facilities are available, including meeting rooms for local groups, and a coffee shop with exhibition space. A new service from Worcestershire Libraries means that people can now visit when staff are not on duty, if, for example, work or other commitments mean that they can't visit during usual opening hours. The library has attractive gardens maintained by a group of volunteers. Other volunteers are helping to conserve, catalogue and promote historic collections donated or collected over the years. The library is a welcoming community resource. It now also shares premises with the job centre.

Having a public library in Malvern at all was at one time a highly controversial issue. The first Public Library Act was passed in 1850 and was followed by a succession of Acts to encourage towns to establish libraries in their areas. J. W. Lucas, the librarian at Malvern, compiled a book published in 1940 and still available in the reference section. It details the history of how Malvern came eventually to build a library for public use.

Before the end of the nineteenth century nearly four hundred towns (many smaller than Malvern) had adopted the Public Library Acts. Malvern had not. In the mid-1890s some residents came up with a project to pool their own books. Thirty-two people joined the scheme, 10,000 volumes were contributed and the Malvern Federated Library was born. It continued until 1902 by which time it had demonstrated the need for a library. Many of its members were involved in lobbying for a public library for all. Reasons for having a library included:

> a comprehensive source for instruction, elevation, relaxation, information and general improvement calculated to amply repay to all classes the slight incidence of rate.

Those opposed to the library said that the district was too scattered to make library provision possible, the expense would be prohibitive and the proposal would result in the socialization of Malvern.

The debates rumbled on. Eventually, conscious that Malvern was behind the times, the now considerable lobby made the case that

> A public library is as necessary for healthy mental life as was good sanitation for physical well-being.

The rate would be no more than 1 penny in the pound, supporters declared that a public library was 'a standard of the public spirit of the place'.

The Council agreed, a committee was re-constituted, including co-opted members, gifts were encouraged and temporary premises with a librarian were established at No 7, the Exchange. There was still some opposition.

Andrew Carnegie, the American industrialist and philanthropist, a Scot by birth, offered £5,000 for a building on condition that the Library Acts were adopted. There was still some opposition. A deputation of ratepayers supported by the vicar of Malvern lobbied in favour, and, encouraged by the surveyor Henry Maybury, included the views of working men, stonemasons and carpenters. And the leaders of the free churches agreed too.

The Council meeting on 28 July 1903 was decisive. It was agreed to accept Carnegie's offer.

Sir Henry Lambert offered the land in Graham Road. Charles Dyson Perrins (who was originally not in favour of a public library) proposed that a lecture hall be included and offered a further £3,000. So there were funds for building and furnishing the premises.

Henry Crouch, a successful architect, had designed many public buildings including Worthing Public Library. He won the competition overseen by RIBA to design the library at Malvern. The builder James Herbert of Wolverhampton won the contract to build and Sir Henry laid the foundation stone on 5 February 1905. There was a public luncheon at the Imperial Hotel, a lecture and a procession to the library site for the ceremony. The local papers assessed that a crowd of five thousand was present.

The library was formally opened on 18 May 1906.

The *Worcester Herald* declared that the library was 'bringing the best books of the best authors within the reach of the poorest.'

When discussing the seventies, historian Gill Holt said,

> I think we all used the library. That was a big thing in Malvern. It was a very good facility. It was used a lot.

A small photograph is currently displayed on the wall in the current reference area. It shows the interior of the library around the time Michael Dowty took his photograph of the still handsome exterior frontage. The parquet floor has been replaced by carpet, more comfortable for the young to sit or crawl on and much easier to clean. The then modern fixed island shelving made the space less adaptable than the current moveable units we find today, but they were in-keeping with contemporary interior

(Opposite page) illus. 39. Laying the library foundation stone (image courtesy of Brian Iles)

furniture designs and would have provided a bright, modern environment. There have been many changes in the library over the years. You can see some of them on the photographs which are kept in the collection of historic materials.

(Above) illus. 40. The Library in late 60s/early 70s (image courtesy of Malvern Library)

(*Opposite page*) illus. 41. Malvern Bookshop and entrance to Priory (D150)

Books and Bookshops

If you could not find what you wanted to read in Malvern Library or if you wanted to buy your own copy of a new or even old out-of-print or antiquarian book then Malvern was, and still is, able to provide plenty of choice.

THE MALVERN BOOKSHOP

The Malvern Book Shop in Abbey Road down the steps to the Priory has been trading since 1954. Founded by the Lechmere family who also published local history books, it has had only three previous owners. It has slightly reduced its selling space in recent years but still carries a huge and varied stock which often attracts visitors in search of particular books and subjects as well as those simply wanting to browse. Its website provides a tour of the premises.

THE PRIORY BOOKSHOP

In 1971 Edith Newth kept the Priory Bookshop and stationers on

Abbey Stylists
THE
MALVERN
BOOKSHOP
R.A.H. LECHMERE
MALVERN PRIORY
WELCOMES VISITORS

Belle Vue Terrace where the present Picnic Box Café is now. Like Iapetus, its neighbour in the arcade, it still has its original 1930s window frames. One of the waitresses said that her grandmother had enjoyed working in the bookshop. She had later worked for Boots which also used to have a lending library.

W. H. SMITH'S

W. H. Smith was and is a few doors along. It has an attractive frontage where, on either side of the premises, if you look up, you will see coloured tile decorative features (dating probably from the 1920s) advertising maps and postcards. This site was originally occupied by the post office run by Henry Cross who also ran the printers, stationers and bookshop and a branch of Mudie's Select Library.

A BBC4 programme, *The Beauty of Books*, broadcast in August 2021 proclaimed: 'In the 1970s Britain was in love with paperback reading.'

Book sales were booming. Best-sellers in 1971 included *The Day of the Jackal* by Frederick Forsyth, *Nemesis* by Agatha Christie, Terry Pratchett's *The Carpet People*, *The Moon's a Balloon* by actor David Niven and Spike Milligan's *Adolph Hitler: My Part in His Downfall*. The successful series for children of Mr Men books started in 1971 with the publication of the first one, *Mr Tickle*. Fifty years later, 85 million copies of the Mr Men books have been sold. Germaine Greer's *The Female Eunuch* appeared in paperback in this year too.

(*Above*) illus. 43. W. H. Smith's advert (JC102)

(*Opposite page*) illus. 42. Belle Vue Terrace (D141)

DISPENSING SAVORY MOORE CHEMISTS
TO LET
THE PRIORY BOOKSHOP
Chartered Surveyors
283 6055
Huddersfield Building Society
BURGH & CO
FABRICS
JFK634H

Today, W. H. Smith still stocks a wide range of books with best sellers often at discounted prices or as special promotions – something not possible in 1971 when the Net Book Agreement, which had been set up in the UK and Ireland between publishers and booksellers to fix the price of books to be sold to the public, was still in place. It ended in 1997 and many independent booksellers went out of business. A recent innovation in some bookshops is a display of books promoted by TikTok, the social media site, with the banner 'TikTok made me buy it' aimed at the site's users. One prolific American writer Colleen Hoover is very popular according to staff at the Malvern Smith's branch although the range of authors is wide and will vary according to the site's users' comments. A bookseller in Foyles in Birmingham reported that Dostoevsky was currently trending (January 2023) and that the promotion had brought in new buyers from a younger age group.

Illus. 44. TikTok books promotion.

The Malvern Book Co-operative at St Ann's Road has an excellent selection of books and, what's more, can often get a book on request by the following day if in stock at their supplier. Malvern readers also have a good choice from the books at Oxfam and from bookshops run by Amnesty in Edith Walk and St Richard's Hospice at Malvern Link.

Chapter Three
Communications

The Post Office and Telephones

The Post Office was built in 1935 on the site of the former Vicarage and backing on to the original Cecilia Hall, now in Church Street. It is also now the home of Thorntons, selling cards, gifts, ice-cream and chocolates. Dowty has several photos of postmen including the one with a trolley on page 95.

The year 1971 saw the first strike by postal workers who were seeking a 19.5 per cent pay rise. Delayed letters were stamped with a message 'Postage delayed by Post Office strike 1971.' At the time a first-class stamp cost 5d (3p after decimalisation), 2nd class was 4d (later 2 1/2p).

The building facing Church Street with huge windows was once the telephone exchange. In the days before mobile phones, it was not uncommon for people not to have a phone in their own house. But for some people a telephone was essential. Dr Harcup in his early days as a GP talked about the situation:

Our wives were receptionists and, of course, they took telephone calls at night. The calls to the practice were diverted to whoever was on-call and then I would have to report back to Mary because there were no mobile phones in those days if I was out. Of course, looking back on it, it was relatively dangerous doing night-calls because we carried not just prescription pads but morphine and pethidine. And quite strong drugs.

There had been a telegraph office in Malvern in the 1870s and by 1895 the National Telephone Company had offices in Church Street with a public phone in 1906. Five years later the Post Office took over responsibility for it. There was no automatic way of storing phone numbers. They had to be recorded manually. Printed telephone directories for specific areas were produced for subscribers and were available (unless removed by persons unknown!) in public phone boxes and libraries. Yellow Pages were produced with business numbers listed. Phone numbers were otherwise obtained by dialling a telephone operator and getting through to Directory Enquiries.

Phone boxes often displayed important numbers inside. The telephone service was still a national service but was privatised in 1984. Some old phone boxes can still be seen. Some have been given other uses, for example housing for defibrillators. The national collection of phone boxes and a recreated exchange can be visited at Avoncroft Museum near Bromsgrove. In Malvern the box at the bus shelter at the end of

(*Top*) illus. 46. Postman in Church Street (D021)

(*Above*) illus. 47. Victorian Post Box St Andrews Road junction (D054)

(*Opposite page*) illus. 45. Post Office (D030)

Belle Vue Terrace has been accompanied by a graphic image of Elgar with a mobile phone.

The design of phones changed considerably over time and moved from dial to keypad as the slim line TRIM phone developed during the sixties. The famous painting by David Hockney, Mr and Mrs Clark and Percy, was made in 1970–71. Beside them stands a very stylish white traditionally shaped telephone with a dial.[2]

In an 1891 business directory, what later became the telephone exchange building in Malvern was listed as Cecilia Hall. Built by Haddon's in 1877, it housed the music business of William Haynes and Co., Musical Instruments Merchants. A detailed description and illustration can be found in the British Library reprint edition which is useful for other information about the later Victorian period. Below in the basement part of the same premises down Church Hill is now a bar and music venue, the Old Con, in the former Conservative Association Social Club. According to the *Gazette* it is about to be re-launched under a new name, OCC, as a 'multi-purpose venue including a sports bar, nightclub and an exclusive private dining area'.

(*Above*) illus. 48. Telephone Kiosk in Grange Road (D154)

(*Opposite page*) illus. 49. *Malvern Gazette* office (D096)

THE MALVERN GAZETTE, ABOVE 75 CHURCH STREET

The offices of the *Malvern Gazette* were up the steps near where Priory

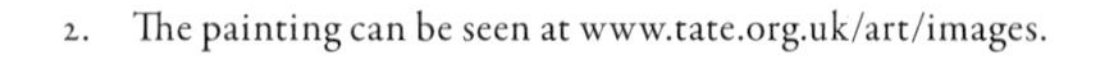
2. The painting can be seen at www.tate.org.uk/art/images.

DING SOCIETY
ON
MALVERN GAZETTE
St George's
DRY CLEANERS
ST. GEORGE'S
WORCESTER CHARTER FESTIVAL
Souvenir Issue
RVEYORS
Estate Agents
AFK 684C

Hairdressers are now. In 1971 the newspaper was a broadsheet with a wide and often detailed coverage of local activities, including black and white photographs. It also covered the main issues of the day with articles on the proposed entry to the Common Market, Comprehensive Education and the introduction of North Sea Gas. It, like many local papers, carried advertisements from the big commercial companies, sometimes full pages, for example, for supermarkets, to small ads from private individuals selling goods or services (For Sale or Wanted) and a variety of Situations Vacant for employment in the Malvern and Worcester area. Job advertisements were allowed to specify the gender of applicants. Women were usually required for retail or office work – one advert showed a young woman using a computer in the accompanying photo. Coverage of agricultural issues and shows was more extensive than it is today. The *Gazette* offices later moved down to Broads Bank.

Newspapers, Stationery and Office Equipment

CAMERON'S, 97 CHURCH STREET

Cameron's at 97 Church Street sold a wide range of stationery and artists materials and local maps In the 1930s it had been Winifred's selling wool and needlework materials and lingerie. A 1939 advert added that maid's uniforms were a speciality. Cameron's was there until the 1990s. It later became St. Michael's Hospice Shop.

MALVERN GA

and Ledbury Reporter

Despite plea for reduction

No change in theatre trust rent

Exhibiting in London

To discuss bus subsidy again

COLOUR TV's

SONY 13" PORTABLE £192.59

HITACHI 15" - £199

HITACHI 17" - £214

FERGUSON 19" - £239.15

COLOUR RENTAL

From £1 WEEKLY

Initial payment £26

WIRELESS SUPPLY DEPOT

WORCESTER ROAD, MALVERN

DISABLED GUESTS

LIFE IN GREECE

CHILDREN HELPING CHILDREN

Longer and longer . . .

GARDEN PARTY

Come and see

The time machine.

TISSOT

Stockist

I. PARRY

WATCHMAKER & JEWELLER

115 CHURCH STREET

(Left) illus. 50. The *Gazette* in 1971 (JC Courtesy of Brian Iles and the *Malvern Gazette*)

W. H. SMITH

(*See illus. 25. Morley's newspaper bundles,* D010, *p.58.*)

In 1971 W. H. Smith occupied the same premises as it does today (see also above Books and Bookshops). There were changes in the newspaper business this year. The *Daily Sketch* ended after 62 years and the *Daily Mail* issued its last broadsheet and became a tabloid. The *Daily Express* cost 3p. Decorative advertising tiles are above on the side of the shop front. The premises had been in Victorian times the site of the post office and a library.

CHAPMAN'S OFFICE EQUIPMENT SUPPLIES, 8 BELLE VUE TERRACE

This would have been a useful location for such a business, near to solicitors, estate agents and other commercial premises. It provided a wide range of stationery and typewriters. At the beginning of this century the business here was known as Severn Office Systems. It is now Deja Vue St Richards Hospice Dress Agency.

Arnold & Greenhalgh
(Fabrications) Ltd
AA
WORCESTER GARAGES
3042
HA
ABBEY

(*Above*) illus. 52. Midland Red Depot (D117)

(*Opposite page*) illus. 51. Girls and buses (D075)

Chapter Four
Transport

Buses and Trains

Lots of buses appear on Michael Dowty's photographs, far more than you see around today.

Karen Hill said:

> The Midland Red bus depot was where B&Q is today but in between times it was Kwik Save supermarket where everything was sold from delivery boxes that had arrived at the store.

The former bus depot would have provided plenty of space for this enterprise. The photographs show the buses bearing several different numbers of routes and destinations and bus stops and bus shelters, one of which still exists today backing on to Rose Bank Gardens. Some show the traffic congestion which they added to at the top of the island.

In the photograph on page 103, people are queueing at the top of the Priory steps to get on the bus to take them home. They do not look particularly happy. The title of the photograph is taken from the little sign by the bus door exhorting would be passengers to do just that. Bus passes which exist today were not, as far as I know, available. Before Pay-as-you-enter was introduced, most buses had not only a driver but also a conductor who came round, took fares and issued tickets. Passengers did not have to queue in all weathers. They simply got on and the bus moved off. Pay-as-you-enter did away with the need for a conductor. In some areas of the country, other, quicker punch cards and machines were introduced. The card was bought in advance so queues were shorter. Was there a similar scheme on Midland Red buses? The looks on the faces of those waiting in the queue suggest that there wasn't.

(*Opposite page*) illus. 53. Boarding pay-as-you-enter bus (148D).

When decimal currency was introduced (D-day Monday 15 February 1971) Midland Red put an advert in the *Malvern Gazette* of 11 February:

> Buses are going over to decimal fares on Sunday 21st of February. Before 21st Please try to pay your fare in old coinage. New coinage will be accepted only in multiples of 2 1/2p.
>
> From 21st Please try to pay your fare in new coinage. Old coinage will be accepted in multiples of 6d. Thank you for your co-operation.

There were also to be fare increases of one new penny at busy times of the day ('Commuters hit by new fares rise') announced by West Midlands

8'-6"
8'-6"
A449
A4105
ABBEY HOTEL
PAY AS YOU
ENTER
Midland Red

Traffic Commissioners. In April the Council expressed concern over the proposal by Midland Red to cut some rural services.

Transport issues were important to school children and their parents. If you had passed your 11-plus exam in Malvern, you may have got a place in a grammar school in Worcester or Hanley Castle. Comprehensive schools were still not the norm here (although some local authorities had had them for years) and as the debate about introducing them continued, the *Malvern Gazette* reported (29/4/1971) an upsurge in interest in the flourishing local private sector. Physically getting to your grammar school could mean that your day probably started with one or possibly two forms of public transport. Although more people owned cars and more women drove too, the car does not seem to have been routinely used to take children to school. Sometimes there were dedicated school buses. One school boy described his journey to Hanley Castle Grammar School:

> From eleven to eighteen I had to take the coach from Malvern Link to Hanley Castle Grammar School and back, having to walk down the hill to catch it, sitting in the back seats with Nick, Timothy and Tony, where we would chat and be silly, progressively over the years getting bigger and smuttier.

Karen Hill described her journey to Worcester Grammar School for Girls at Spetchley where the Sixth Form College is now:

Illus. 54. Train arriving at busy platform (D036)

> Most of us travelled by train either from Great Malvern or Malvern Link. In the morning we were crammed in with the general public in a nine-carriage train. In the afternoon it was a three-carriage train with the public and those of us from the Kings School, the Royal Grammar School, the Convent and Alice Ottley as well as from Worcester Grammar School for Girls . . . our boaters tended to be quite blackened by travelling by train.
>
> The head, who regarded the Malvern pupils as county children who were there by invitation, complained about the boaters, the blocking of the pavement outside Foregate Street station while waiting for buses to take them on to school, and their late arrival. When the fully loaded double decker Midland Red got to the bottom of the London Road, we all had to get off and walk up the hill and board it at the top. This was repeated until we arrived at school. The only good thing about this was that all the Malvern train people were fully aware of how many river terraces there were which really impressed the geography staff!

Young people often depended on public transport for access to leisure activities too. Rock concerts at the Winter Gardens attracted the young from far and wide. One woman told me in the now often tranquil Priory Park about those heady days of her youth. For a particular concert she had come by bus with friends from Worcester. She wore a grass skirt for the concert. Losing all sense of time, she missed the last bus back so still wearing the grass skirt, had to walk back all the way home.

Sean Austin was from Worcester too. He recalled visits to Malvern as a young boy:

> Malvern to me was our playground when we were kids in the summer holidays. I remember getting on the train at Shrub Hill with six or seven of my friends from the local estate and we'd be on our own – age ranges six to eight years old – and we'd get the train through to Great Malvern with the intention of going up the hills for the day.

(*Top*) illus. 56. Graham Road free of cars 7.20am. (D024)

(*Above*) illus. 57. Graham Road with cars (D132)

(*Opposite page*) illus. 55. Parking in Church Street (D043)

Cars and Delivery Vans

While buses could sometimes contribute to traffic congestion, Michael Dowty's photographs show other traffic issues. Delivery vans can still hinder traffic on Church Street as they did in 1971 and today some of them are much larger. The popularity of online ordering has meant that we also see more home delivery services on the roads and parking in unexpected places.

On-street parking is still an attractive option for many today, in spite of some time restrictions. Double yellow lines were introduced in the early 1960s. Michael's photographs of Graham Road without parked cars in the early morning on 30 July contrasts with that later in the day when parking seemed almost to be bumper to bumper.

The *Gazette* of 17 June reported on traffic problems highlighted in a

RTON ALE
Wonderloaf
St George's
DRY CLEANERS
PETTIFORS
HOUSE
922 CUY

survey by Malvern Young Socialists. They interviewed 513 shoppers and thirty-two traders about what conditions were like and what could be done to improve them. Some thought Church Street should be closed to traffic, others that parking should be banned or that it should be made one-way. Problems raised included the danger of traffic to pedestrians, complaints about fumes and noise making shopping unpleasant. The suggestion that the Priory churchyard should become a car park met with 'considerable adverse comment'.

The results of the survey were sent to the Council. Malvern UDC Surveyor said that the Young Socialists had produced a very thorough and interesting report.

(*Opposite page*) illus. 58. Abbey Gateway (D080)

THE ABBEY GATEWAY

The 1971 photo shows that cars were allowed to go under the Abbey Gateway. The Gateway has a long history. It was probably built in wood around the time the monastery was founded in 1085 and replaced in stone about 1480. Strictly speaking it is the Priory Gateway as the 'abbey' was a priory of Westminster Abbey. The Priory covered a large area surrounded by a wall. It would have included not only monastic buildings such as an infirmary, cloisters, almonry but also gardens, orchards and a fish pond. The gateway was staffed by a janitor to control access. Following the dissolution under Henry VIII in 1539, most of the buildings were sold off. The people of Malvern bought the Priory Church to be their own

8 FT. 6 INS.
HEAD-ROOM

parish church. The gatehouse too survived. Bought eventually by the Mason Family, it was later used by William Mayo for his estate agent's business. Other uses over time included a magistrate's court, a fruit vegetable and game shop and an architect's office. The young J. M. W. Turner visited and sketched the gateway in the summer of 1793 and later in the 1830s made it into the famous painting now in the Whitworth Gallery of Manchester University.[3] Prints were made and the engraver, J. Horsburgh, added a bolt of lightning for dramatic effect.

Illus. 59. *Malvern Abbey and Gate, Worcestershire, 1832.* After Joseph Mallord William Turner. Part of *Picturesque Views in England and Wales.*

The Abbey Hotel used the Gatehouse as staff quarters for some years and the architect and friend of Edward Elgar, Troyte Griffiths had his practice here. The North Front was restored in 1891.

Traffic was allowed through the Gateway for many years although some damage to the stonework occurred from time to time. A 4 miles an hour restriction was put in place with a height restriction of 8ft 6ins. The idea of closing the road was discussed but was not popular. In June 1979 a Wall's delivery van tried to go through. It was 10ft 6ins high. The *Gazette* published a photograph with the van firmly wedged under the arch which was badly damaged and not just superficially. Repairs to make the building safe and put right the damage came to £10,000. The road was permanently closed to traffic and the building was handed over to Malvern Museum of Local History where you can now see more

3. See the Turner painting at www.whitworth.manchester.ac.uk/collections, search for Malvern (title of painting: Great Malvern Abbey).

information about it. As a Grade II* listed building the Gateway is itself the largest exhibit the Museum has.

Petrol Stations

The garage in the photograph overleaf was a traditional Shell garage in 1971. The following month saw the arrival of the first self-service petrol station in Malvern belonging to the same company. The *Malvern Gazette* (26/8/1971) ran an article with a large advertisement for the Bowman and Acock Sunny Lodge Self Service Station which sold various grades of BP petrol. Motorists were offered information on how easy the system was to use. The advert included a cartoon of young women in very short skirts and high boots, one of them holding a petrol pump nozzle. The information box displayed the words:

> Belinda and Julia will show you how easy it is to serve yourself.

While hemlines rose and fell and fluctuated over the years, self-service petrol at the pumps took off to become the norm. Petrol prices in the illustration are not easy to read and seem to depend on the grade 2 to 5 star. (Leaded petrol was not banned until 2000 but had begun to be phased out in the 1980s.) There was an opening offer of 2p off per gallon for all grades . . . as well as Quad Green Shield Stamps. The average cost

(*Left*) illus. 60. Bowman and Acock (D004)

of petrol in 1971 was 34p a gallon. Today there are an increasing number of electric vehicles on the road (*Guardian* 20/10/2021 for UK plans). The drivers of electric cars can use one of a number of charging points situated in public car parks.

Chapter Five
Public Services

Gas

The West Midlands Gas Board was established in 1948 as were other area Boards. The Malvern Improvement Act of 1851 had led to the establishment of Town Commissioners to set up and oversee various services. They issued contracts for the building of a Gas Works and one was erected at the junction of Pickersleigh and Sherrards Green Roads. By 1856 the Gas Works was ready and there was a celebratory beacon lit on the hills. Five hundred houses could be lit by gas and two hundred gas lamps provided lighting for all the older streets in the town. Many gas lights still exist.

In 1962 the first surveys for oil and gas in the North Sea began. Natural gas was found and plans drawn up to convert from town gas (containing 45 per cent hydrogen, fast burning) to Natural Gas (also called North Sea Gas) which contained 95 per cent methane and burned more slowly. Conversion started in 1968 with lots of press coverage explaining what would take place. In 1971 it was Malvern's turn.

'Natural gas comes to town' heralded the *Gazette* headline with photographs of advice sessions, workmen digging holes and a woman standing by a gas cooker. The article continued:

> A heavily armed regiment of gas fitters, gas converters, technicians, conversion officers and others invaded Malvern on Monday as conversion to North Sea Gas got underway . . . Housewives and householders in nearly 3,000 gas consuming homes were knocked up at about 8am by workmen who had come to turn off the supplies.
>
> The operation is down to a fine art. There are home service girls to iron out any problems – special recipes are even available to help the housewife with her family menu while her cooker is being converted – and a mobile inquiry unit has been stationed on the car park at Link Top.

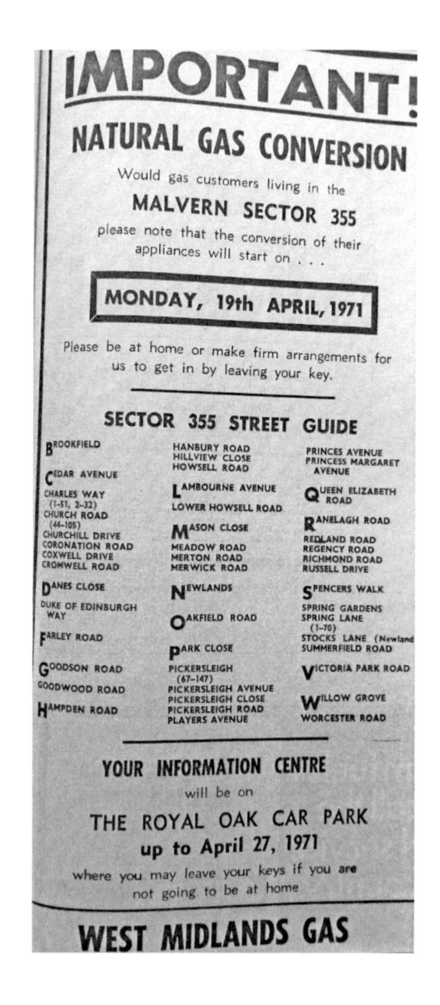

The work was planned to take four weeks (*Malvern Gazette* 25/3/1971 and 1/4/1971).

Maureen and Christopher Davis remembered what happened. Maureen explained:

> I was expecting my second child at the time. I'd got a boy two and a half years old. We had gas fires in three of the rooms and a gas cooker which meant the floors had to come up in each of these rooms. The only room which didn't have

(*Left*) illus. 61. Information in the newspaper. (JC30 Courtesy of *Malvern Gazette*)

the floor up was the bathroom. The hallway also had the floor up. So I was there with all these gaps in the floor with a two-and-a-half-year-old running around and expecting. It was quite stressful really . . .

Christopher added:

> They did a test at the start. They had to make absolutely sure there were no leaks anywhere and of course being an old building, when they actually came to test for leaks, they put a plug thing in and if the pressure drops, it shows there is a leak somewhere and of course being old gas pipes, then apparently with North Sea Gas, it was more likely to cause trouble than it had done with the old Town Gas.
>
> Maureen said: Because you couldn't smell it. We could only cook on low pressure on the gas stove, so I was very thankful because I had a pressure cooker which speeded things up. I couldn't really use the oven at all. Just the top, the hob.

Electricity

The M.E.B. (Midlands Electricity Board) showrooms were on the corner of St Ann's Road and the Worcester Road. In 1971 the M.E.B. was responsible for the electricity supply for a large part of the Midlands. Most towns had a showroom. Here you could pay your electricity bill which came through the post, discuss anything to do with the domestic supply (many

ERN MINI MARKET
OXFAM GIFT SHOP
WHITBREAD
UNICORN
ELECTRICITY
ELECTRICITY SERVICE CENTRE
BARCLAYS
HARPER LAYTON
LADIES & GENTLEMENS HAIRDRESSER

(*Top*) illus. 63. The electricity works – boilers and refuse destructor furnaces. (Courtesy of Malvern Museum)

(*Above*) illus. 64. Lucy Box (JC)

(*Opposite page*) illus. 62. M.E.B. 6.45am (D009)

people had electricity meters where people put money in the slot to pay for electricity as they used it), or look at a range of products and discuss them with a showroom assistant before deciding whether to purchase or not. As has been noted above, at the time freezers were becoming more popular. A twin tub washing machine which combined the washing and spin-drying function cost around £85, an automatic (still not yet a common appliance) about £105 or more and a Russell Hobs kettle £9.

The M.E.B. was established in 1947 and was what was known as a 'public sector utilities company'. Its role was to buy electricity from the electricity generator and, before changes in 1998, distribute it and sell it throughout the West Midlands area.

Malvern wasn't keen on the idea of electricity at first . . .

'We don't want it' was the general sentiment at a public meeting in 1900 attended by 1,500 people. There was much discussion and heckling, resulting in the turning down of the proposal that the Council should supply electricity. But in 1903 Mr Maybury the surveyor produced a scheme for the generation of electricity from a 'refuse destructor' which could be built at the old gas works – an early example of waste management.

The idea was accepted, a chimney was built and 15 miles of cable laid. But by 1906 only 112 people had subscribed to the power source. But it was a start! The green metal structure, known as a Lucy Box, on St Ann's Road was an early electrical distribution box.

Water

(*Opposite page*) illus. 65.
Street cleaning vehicle (D023)

Doctor Green in his last annual report in 1972 as Medical Officer of Health informed Malvern District Council about water supplies in 1971:

> A deep borehole at Bromsberrow sunk in new red sandstone provides an abundant and good water supply. It is not contaminated in anyway. Water is also collected from the hills in the reservoir near British Camp but this is now more of a standby. Only a few houses are supplied with water from shallow wells. Samples are sent to the laboratory for analysis from time to time.

In the past, Malvern houses sometimes sank their own wells or made use of water from wells on their property. Today people still collect water straight from some of the hills, especially from the tap on the island at Belle Vue. All public sources are tested and signs put up if water is unfit for drinking.

Refuse and Cleaning Public Facilities

Doctor Green also reported:

> Refuse was removed to Guarlford sewerage works by means of tipping. Street sweeping was carried out in the central area daily, elsewhere weekly.

National Westminster Bank

Street sweeping took place in the early morning – Dowty has two photographs one putting the time at 7.30am of a vehicle possibly clearing a drain and one sweeping. Another shows an early morning shopkeeper sweeping the pavement outside his shop (*see above – Dewhurst's Illus. 16*). The children's paddling pool and sand pit were also cleaned at the start of the day.

Public Lavatories

The public lavatories next to the theatre complex in Priory Road and near to the Park have recently been completely renovated.

Goad's 1971 plan shows two public loos near the top of Edith Walk, 'lav' on the plan. The Public Health Act of 1936 made the provision of public lavatories optional and at one time the District Council proposed closing Malvern's facilities. One of the Edith Walk loos was closed but was not quite lost to the public thanks to an idea from the creative puppet enthusiast and artist Denis Neal in 1999. The former public loo became the Theatre of Small Convenience. It was beautifully decorated inside and could hold an audience of about a dozen people. Run as an independent and not for profit project, both amateur and professional performances took place in what the Guinness Book of Records in 2002 described as the smallest theatre in the world. One review called the theatre 'Beautiful, wonderful and gloriously surreal.'

(*Above*) illus. 67. Exterior of the Theatre of Small Convenience

(*Opposite page*) illus. 66.
Priory Park paddling pool 9.30 am (D045)

It was still open in 2017 when its creator retired. Now recorded as 'temporarily closed', the recent tenant was the Warwickshire College Group, the lease ending in December 2022. Malvern Hills District Council owns the theatre and its future was recently reported (16/3/2023) as in doubt. For reasons of a low EPC rating, it cannot, it was said, legally be re-let. The Council was reported to be reviewing its options. At the time of writing, a campaign to save the theatre has started on social media. The small photograph was taken at the end of 2022 when an inspection of the condition of the interior was being carried out.

(*Above*) illus. 68. Interior of the Theatre of Small Convenience

Chapter Six
Banks and Building Societies

Banks

BARCLAYS BANK, 2 WORCESTER ROAD

(See illus. 28. Burleys and Barclays Bank, D101, p.67.)

Until recently Barclays Bank occupied the once famous Royal Library built in classical style for reading and to provide a leisurely, relaxing environment for visitors. The building was adapted for use as Barclays Bank in 1930. In 2021 Barclays put up a notice to customers about closing the branch and told the *Gazette* (12/5/2021) that it now had only fifty regular customers, footfall had reduced by 22 per cent over the previous two years and 86 per cent used alternative ways of banking. It was no longer viable to keep it open. There was considerable public anxiety over the closure of yet another bank in the vicinity, including objections from the local MP who banked there. Some reports gave the figure of eighty users. In 1971 most banks had thriving branches in small towns and many customers, business or individuals appreciated and took for granted the personal service received. The first UK cash machine was in use at a Barclays branch in North London in 1967 but there have been other claims for early online ATMs including IBM and Lloyds. In 1971 technology had not developed to make on-line banking from home possible. Few offices had computers and mobile phones and home computers did not exist as they do today.

(*Opposite page*) illus. 69. Lloyds Bank (D196)

LLOYDS BANK, BELLE VUE TERRACE

Lloyds Bank was built on the site of the Crown Hotel which became Graefenberg House when Dr Wilson set up his water cure treatment there in 1842. The bank, a dignified and impressive building with the initials LB entwined above the door, was designed by J. A. Chatwin in the 1890s. This architect had a contract with Lloyds to design their premises and there are similar ones in Wolverhampton and Birmingham.

MIDLAND BANK, 1 CHURCH STREET

The top of Church Street was once known as Paradise Row. Most of the properties were built as houses with names rather than numbers. An 1880s photo taken from the top of the Priory tower shows the shops here. The properties, set back from the road, could be extended forwards to become shops and businesses.

The HSBC was originally the London and Midland Bank, later the Midland, on the site of Edith House and the later Lewis and Son's Café

Royal. The bank was built in 1920-1. Set back from the main row of shops, its position may have made it difficult to photograph because of the road junction and traffic.

NATIONAL WESTMINSTER BANK, 19–21 CHURCH STREET

On the steeper part of Church Street in a commanding position stands the now former Tourist Information Centre which is now located next to Lyttleton Well, half way down the hill. The premises were in 1971 occupied by the National Westminster Bank and later the Leeds Permanent Building Society in the eighties and nineties. During the extensive renovations to turn the building into a shop in 2022, it was necessary to remove the former strong room door. It had been left open and revealed the mechanisms which had once secured it. The door seems to have been very much built as an integral part of the strong room design and proved to be difficult to remove and demolish. During his lunch break,

National Westminster Bank
SWEETS
TOBACCO
CHURCH ST
BYB 380R
CNP 156H

one of the team took a photograph of the door while still firmly *in situ*. It has now been safely removed and renovations continued for the new occupants, Crew Clothing Company.

The National Westminster Bank building at the Graham Road cross roads is not as old as it looks. It was built in a classically influenced style in the 1930s and was, until 1970, the National Provincial Bank which had announced its merger with the National Westminster two years earlier. It closed in 2018/19. The building has since reinvented itself as a cocktail bar with live music on some evenings. There are photographs from the Nat West Archive of the former bank's interior just inside the entrance. One review praises the bar for its 'series of Malvern themed drinks, each inspired by a piece of the town's history.'

(*Above*) illus. 72. Strongroom door demolition (JC66)

(*Opposite page*) illus. 73. Traffic lights and National Westminster Bank (D016)

(*Previous pages*) illus. 70. Belle Vue Terrace Bus Shelter (142D)and illus. 71. View down Church Street (D098)

Building Societies

WORCESTER BUILDING SOCIETY, 13 WORCESTER ROAD

It made good sense to have building societies in the vicinity of estate agents and there were several in the area. The Worcester was established in 1859 and later joined to the Redditch which became part of the Midshires Building Society formed in 1975. The Bridgewater Building Society was about to take over the vacant premises at number 19 Worcester Road. It joined as the Birmingham and Bridgewater Building Society and became the Birmingham Midshires in 1986. By 2022 John Goodwin Estate Agents

Nationa
We
minster Bank

occupied the premises at No 13. Estate agents still dominate this area. The main buildings containing these premises were once the White Horse Hotel, York House and Beauchamp Terrace. Other building societies were the Gloucester and the Huddersfield (indicated on a small sign above Edith Newth's bookshop on Belle Vue Terrace.)

Building Societies were able to offer banking services in the 1980s following legislation of 1986 and further changes allowing them to de-mutualise later in the decade. More changes have taken place in the twenty-first century.

The history of building societies in the UK is complex. Wikipedia contains text and charts which are interesting and show changes of ownership. Individual building societies and banks often include their history on or from their websites.

Credit and Debit Cards

Today we can use on-line banking services and make use of debit and credit cards ('plastic') to make often even small payments live or on-line, increasingly scanning a code from a mobile phone. These methods have grown in popularity during the recent Covid pandemic and have been accompanied by a growth of warehouse-based supply companies now dominated by Amazon and a growth in collection points and delivery firms to get goods to the purchasers. At the time of writing, there is discussion about where this will lead following changes in the current economic conditions and personal financial circumstances and an awareness of issues surrounding consumerism and the transport of goods in the light of climate concerns.

Estate Agents

J. G. LEAR, 71 CHURCH STREET

J. G. Lear Estate Agents had their offices in the small classical style building which is now the Priory Salon. One of the oldest businesses as auctioneers and estate agents in Malvern, it is described in the 1891 directory as having been in existence for many years. Its display of photographs of property for sale was near the steps leading up to the *Gazette* offices and can be seen in the 1971 photograph.

White Seats and Ridley Speight Lear and Lear estate agents were also at 16 Worcester Road.

This business was one of several estate agents in the area in 1971. Others included J. P. Harper Layton (no. 10), Philip Laney and Jolley (no. 12), and G. Herbert Banks (no. 13a).

The average UK house price in 1971 was £5,000.

MALVERN
GAZETTE
FERMOR
ARMS
J G LEAR & SON
ESTATE AGENTS
GUY 5J

(*Opposite page*) illus. 74. Outside the *Gazette* offices (D140)

Chapter Seven
Health

BURROWS, 10 BELLE VUE TERRACE

Burrows Factory was reached via the wide entrance next door to Morley's shop. This was the bottling factory for the water from St Ann's Well collected in tanks to the rear of the then Crown Hotel. In the nineteenth century Burrow's Malvern Waters had great success with their product gaining Royal Warrants and international acclaim.[4] The bottling works closed in the 1950s and the site bought by Clarke Roxborough whose insurance office was at 22–24 Belle Vue Terrace in 1971. The large space has been the Pine Emporium workshop and furniture showroom in the 1980s and 90s and Robson Wards fitted furniture and electrical appliances in 2000s. By 2011 a small arcade of attractive retail shops including Dynastic Art and Zinnia Shoe Boutique. was created but had a fairly short life. Today it is 'be' the Bottling Works at no. 10, creating bottles containing gemstones – there is an interesting leaflet advertising the products. A cycle business is also located here.

4. For further information and their 1882 advertisement, see C. Weaver, and B. Osborne, (1994) *Aquae Malvernensis*.

1971 Health Report

The annual report for 1971 was Dr Green's last report before retirement as Medical Officer of Health. In it he reflected on the changes he had witnessed during his twenty year time in office.

> Over the past twenty years I have through my contacts with the community watched considerable , though undramatic, changes taking place in the way of life and health of the community. When I came here cases of diphtheria had only recently occurred. There were still patients in the old Isolation Hospital. No cases occurred during my tenure of office. Epidemics of poliomyelitis , some of which were very severe, came and went. The disappearance of the disease is almost certainly the result of vaccinations.

He goes on to discuss the decline in tuberculosis and the discovery of new drugs and the development and practice of giving the BCG vaccinations which he says must continue. The main causes of death were disease of heart and blood vessels and other forms of heart disease, cancer, cerebrovascular disease , other diseases of the circulatory system, and pneumonia.

Illus. 75. Bottling works (JC 2022BVbe)

Life Expectancy

The *Guardian* reported (5/5/2004) that average life expectancy in Britain in 1971 was seventy-two years. Estimates in sources vary but in 1971, men might expect to live to sixty-eight (or 69.2) and women to seventy-two (or 75.5). Covid has affected recent statistics but the figures in 2021 were 83.2 for men and 87.9 for women.

Smoking

Cancer is in the list of main causes of death in the 1971 Malvern Health Report (*above*). The Dowty photographs show a few people smoking in the street. In one of the photos several people have pointed out the Embassy cigarette machine is strategically placed inside the entrance to the swimming pool. In 1970 55 per cent of men and 44 per cent of women smoked tobacco, mostly as cigarettes. Research as long ago as 1951 had linked smoking with cancer but it was not until 1971 a health warning was put on cigarette packets:

> WARNING BY HM GOVERNMENT
>
> SMOKING CAN DAMAGE YOUR HEALTH

The charity ASH was formed in 1970 to alert people to the dangers and a decline was noted in statistics for 1980: 42 per cent of men and 37 per cent of women smoked. Sponsorship of sporting and theatrical events by cigarette producers still continued. *Which?* (the magazine of the Consumers Association) published a chart of brands in order of tar content in September 1971 so that readers could see for themselves which was likely to be most harmful. Some people believed that filter tipped cigarettes would protect their health. This was not the case. Embassy cigarettes were overtaken by Players No 6 as the market leader in 1970–71. Eventually because of the decline in UK sales, production was moved by tobacco companies to Germany and Poland.

Vaping (using e-cigarettes) is a comparatively new phenomenon – no tar or carbon monoxide is produced but nicotine is inhaled as a vapour. The NHS suggests vaping might help people to stop smoking but should not be used by existing non-smokers or sold to under eighteen-year-olds. However recent press reports (e.g. *Guardian* 21/2/2023) point out that the fruit and bubble gum 'flavours' are designed to appeal to young people and that the chief medical officer has called for action to reverse the rise in the number of adolescents and children vaping.

Chemists

A. E. BAYLIS, 119 CHURCH STREET

A. E. Baylis chemist's shop was the name at 119 Church Street in 1971.

More recently it was known as Claremont Pharmacy. Baylis's Chemists was listed here in a 1920 directory at premises known as Claremont House. It (and its name) moved to Barnard's Green fairly recently. It's record books go back to the Victorian era and mention many of the visitors to the town. The books are now used as display items in its window. The premises in Church Street were given a complete make-over in 2019–20 and are now the Good Gentlemen Barbershop.

SAVORY AND MOORE, 28 BELLE VUE TERRACE

(*See illus. 42. Belle Vue Terrace, D141, p.91*)

This attractive double fronted shop has a long history which is reflected both inside and outside of the premises. In 1971 the shop was Savory and Moore's chemists and it had been a pharmacist's premises for most of its existence. A few years ago, the shop was called Kalliste, selling women's clothes and jewellery from India. In the 1980s and 90s, the shop was known as Mander's chemists as it had been back in the late nineteenth century, the initial *M* being etched into the window glass. Alfred Mander had been an assistant to the former proprietor Mr Caldwell. An advertisement described some of the services on offer to clients:

> British and foreign dispensing (a qualified pharmacist is always on duty), water beds on hire, the analysis of water etc. conducted in the laboratory, Kodak films and photographic requisites.

The Kodak company was founded in the US in 1892. The famous Brownie camera was introduced in 1900. Chemists and photographers have been related since the early days of photography. In 2017 following the success of his shop in the Shambles, Worcester, jeweller Rodney Randle opened his Malvern shop, Malvern Goldsmiths, making use of the original interior fittings.

BOOTS, 89–91 CHURCH STREET

Fat Face, the popular clothing company chain (named after a mountain ski slope near where it originated) was Boots the Chemists in 1971 and for many years later. The founder Jesse Boot had visited Malvern in the previous century. As well as now having a shop near the top of Church Street (at the time of writing in 2023 for sale as two shops and closing in early March), it has a large shop on the retail park. Above Fat Face, there is still evidence of a possible temperature-controlled room and a hoist for bringing goods up to it for storage. There is also some fine Victorian plasterwork upstairs in this building indicating the tastes of previous occupants. Birthdays (including Thorntons) was here too, selling cards and gifts earlier this century.

CHARLES BISSET, WEST MALVERN

The 1971 photograph taken in West Malvern includes the premises of Charles Bisset. Jeremy Tudge recalled the services the shop provided.

(*Top and centre*) illus. 76. and 77. Earlier interior shop fittings still in place (JC 91 and 92)

(*Above*) illus. 79. Interior plaster coving (image courtesy of Travis Wilson of Fat Face)

(*Opposite page*) illus. 78. Boots (D084)

Boots
DISPENSING CHEMISTS
Boots
ALBION HOUSE
MENS SHOES
LADIES &
LOOK LOBBY SALE
CNP 156H

J. C. Bisset
Optician
Kodak
Kodak

(*Opposite page*) illus. 80.
General view West Malvern Road (D181)

We had an interesting shop in West Malvern. Charlie Bisset was a chemist, but he was a man of many talents. He was also an optician. We used to have our eyes tested there. And glasses were made and fitted there too. He was a photographer who made and took lots and lots of photographs and he sold them as post cards. You can still find Charlie Bisset's post cards in second-hand or antique shops. He used to develop photographs. You could take a film in to him, and he'd develop them and give you the prints. He'd got his own dark room.

Opticians

WALLER AND WALLER, 20–24 WORCESTER ROAD

In 1971 Waller and Waller had their premises between the Carpet Centre and Baxter's. They later moved to the top of Edith Walk where in 1971 had been the insurance offices of Walker, Walker and Roy. Waller and Waller have recently moved out of the attractive premises which, it is thought, still have their original window and door frames. These features will hopefully remain in future when part of the building is likely to be converted to apartments. Waller and Waller are now at Hollands in Graham Road. On a visit to Edith Walk in 2022 I was shown a display case of items from their business in the past. Included were a selection of glass eyes, a case of various lenses used in eye testing and a photograph of the stand at the local show where visitors could get their eyes tested and lenses made for the resulting prescription. There were frames to choose from. On display was a very nice tortoiseshell frame. Wallers still had the remains of the original tortoise shell the frames were cut from but it was not available for display. Happily this truly eye-catching collection has been transferred to the new premises. It is intended to create a window display in future.

Hospitals

MALVERN GENERAL HOSPITAL, LANSDOWNE CRESCENT[5]

Michael Dowty did not take any photographs of the hospital but in 1971 it was still an integral part of the community.

Growth in population and a better understanding of illness, conditions for treatment and medicine meant that Malvern needed more improved facilities for health care than the previous rural hospital could provide. In Lansdowne Crescent some of the once quite grand lodging houses, perhaps as a result of multi occupation, had become run down and difficult to let.

Dyson Perrins owned the freehold and was a benefactor to the public of Malvern, having given funds, for example, towards building the library. He proposed to demolish the houses which backed on to the newly

5. Extracts in this section on the hospital are taken from contributors to the MID oral history project and were first published in: Jan Condon, *A Short History of Malvern Hospitals*. (2022) Jan Condon for the Friends of Malvern Hospital, Malvern.

created (1907) sports club at Manor Park and to use the land to provide a site for a new hospital. He also proposed to pay for the building and the equipping of it.

The hospital was designed by William Henman who was the architect of Birmingham General Hospital and the Royal Victoria Hospital in Belfast. Art Nouveau and Arts and Crafts influences were apparent in the overall design and in many of the decorative details. The hospital was opened in 1911 with a 24-bed capacity, plus a children's ward, operating theatre and outpatient's department. It was staffed by local doctors which meant that the hospital was felt to be very much an integral and trusted part of the community it served. Funds to help the hospital were sometimes given in the form of bed or cot sponsorship. In 1948 after years of charitable funding, the hospital became part of the new National Health Service.

The Malvern in a Day Memories Project includes some accounts of people who worked at the hospital or used its services, mostly in the 1970s. Here are some extracts from what they recorded.

Bill who had epilepsy remembered being taken to the hospital by his mum as a young man in his teens if he had fallen down. He appreciated the ease of getting treatment when he was hurt.

> You could take yourself to the hospital without being referred there by a doctor. The nurses there could treat minor injuries.

Doctor Harcup described the services of the hospital and some of his work there:

> The Community Hospital in Lansdowne Crescent was very active. It had a male ward and a female ward, x-ray facilities and a physiotherapy department and a casualty room and we GPs took over various functions. I looked after emergency surgery cases . . . and I did a lot of surgery so it didn't worry me.

Joy McWhirter was a physiotherapist who qualified at the Royal Victoria Hospital in Belfast. She described how she got a job at the hospital.

> I met Miss Cora Jenkins who was the superintendent physiotherapist and had been there since 1948, the founding of the NHS. I asked if there was a job available of any type that I could do. She asked me questions . . . where I'd qualified and what I'd done and then said, 'Yes, I think we can take you on. Can you start next week?' And that was my interview. So I stayed for about thirty-seven years until I retired.
>
> Some people called it a Cottage Hospital but it was actually a general hospital because we did operations . . . As for the outpatients, we treated the ladies on Mondays, Wednesdays and Fridays and gentlemen on Tuesdays, Thursdays and Saturdays.

The new Malvern Community Hospital opened in 2010 and the old one was offered for sale as a development opportunity. Derelict by 2015, in spite of being in a conservation area, listing was refused and the building was demolished. The care home Windsor Court, carefully designed to fit in with the architecture of the Crescent, now occupies the site.

(*Right*) illus. 81. Hospital demolition (JC)

HARPER LAYTON
ESTATE AGENTS
WHITBREAD
CDD 518B
SPD
72F
ERVICE CENTRE

(*Opposite page*) illus. 82.
Whitbread delivery at old coaching inn (D070)

Chapter Eight
Leisure and Entertainment

Pubs and Off-licences

THE UNICORN, 2 BELLE VUE TERRACE

The pub on the corner of St Ann's Road (locally known as Red Lion Bank) is one of the oldest surviving buildings in Malvern. Remains of its timber framing can be seen outside from the car park and inside the pub itself which is said to date from the sixteenth century. It is a Grade II listed building. There is a plaque on the wall recording visits of C. S. Lewis and J. R. R. Tolkien. Popular today, it has a tiny outside terrace and is backed by a small public car park where once there used to be a number of businesses including a hardware shop, cycle hire business and a hairdressers. Still in the wall of the car park are the remains of a part of the early electricity supply system, known as a Lucy Box.

The 1971 photograph shows the delivery of beer in metal barrels. A fairly recent innovation in the 1960s, they were usually made of stainless steel and were robust and lighter to handle and more manoeuvrable than the previous wooden ones. Some were made by factories in the Midlands (e.g. Joseph Sankey of Bilston). The delivery lorry is from one of the major brewers Whitbread. At the time of the photo, you could get a pint of Whitbread Tankard for 16p. The Whitbread brewery business was founded in 1742 in London.

Across St Ann's Road and a little way along the Worcester Road originally stood another timber framed building which was painted in 1871 by the renowned Worcester artist Benjamin Williams Leader and titled the Old Blacksmith's Shop. Brian Iles has a photograph of the building taken in 1856 (Iles, Brian (2009) Malvern through time. p5) He states that it was demolished soon after that date. It is possible that the Leader painting owed something to the photograph and the rest to his artistic imagination.

(*Above*) illus. 83. The Old Blacksmith's Shop by Benjamin Williams Leader (image from Worcester Museum Collection)

(*Opposite page*) illus. 84. Red Lion Inn (D100)

THE RED LION, 6 ST ANN'S ROAD

The pub is further up the hill from the Unicorn and is set back in a small courtyard where people could sit outside with their drinks. In the 1970s it was owned by Marston's. In the 1990s it was well known for its excellent food. It has had several tenants over the years and has recently reopened. It was flanked in 1971 by antiques/curios shops including Treasure Traders. This shop has recently been a barbers and earlier a Thai restaurant but now looks vacant. Antiques furniture and china at no. 26 is now a private house.

D LION
INN
BREAKFAST
CUY 300B

THE FOLEY ARMS HOTEL

(*Opposite page*) illus. 85. Foley Arms Hotel (D199)

THE CENTRAL HOTEL

The hotel occupied much of the remaining premises on St Ann's Road. It appears on Goad's 1971 plan. This was a Temperance Hotel run for families and those who wanted accommodation in an alcohol-free environment. Ironically, its basement is now occupied by the Malvern Cellar, famous for its comprehensive selection of gins and for its knowledgeable proprietor. The Malvern Book Co-operative occupies some of the ground floor. There is an apartment above.

THE FOLEY ARMS

The cars lined up outside the Foley Arms on Dowty's photograph suggests that motorists may have popped in on their way home from work. Named Downs Hotel after its owner, built to a plan by Samuel Deykes on former Foley land, the hotel opened in 1810. It became a coaching inn. In the 1970s it was managed by Robin Pagan and later bought by the owners of the Savoy in Cheltenham. It has had several managers and owners during its long career and in recent times has been a Best Western. It closed in 2010 but was soon acquired by the J. D. Wetherspoon chain, reopening in December. It is now a popular place to eat and to stay. The interior has a wealth of information and documents about its history displayed for visitors to look at. The hotel has also included a Morgan car as a decorative feature.

THE FERMOR ARMS

(*Opposite page*) illus. 86. Saccone and Speed (D151)

Only just visible on Dowty's photograph (*see illus. 24. D095*) of the Dorothy Café, which was its neighbour, the Fermor Arms was possibly the smallest pub in the county. It was also known as the Hole in the Wall. Built about 1815 on church property, it is first named as the pub in a directory in 1838. Its facilities were said to be basic for many years – no loos sent its clients out into the Priory grounds or a nearby alleyway. In the 1970s Wally and Daisy Jones were landlords. It closed in 1976 as part of the redevelopment of this area.

SACCONE AND SPEED

In the 1971 photo the now Abbey Road Coffee on the right of the steps going down to the Priory was the off-licence Saccone and Speed. Posters in the window show the prices of some of their offers because of tax changes. There was 5p off whisky, gin, brandy, sherry and table wine. Original prices didn't have to be displayed in the window but a bottle of Haigh whisky at the time would have cost £2.53. The shop had a free home delivery service. This area is now a popular place to sit in or outside with a coffee.

SACCONE & SPEED LTD.
SACCONE & SPEED LTD.
S.E.T. DOWN JULY!
OUR PRICES DOWN NOW!
ICE COLD DRINKS
WE OFFER A FREE DELIVERY SERVICE
REDUCED 3p HALF BOTTLES of SMIRNOFF VODKA
REDUCED 3p COURAGE LIGHT & BROWN
IN 6 CAN PACKS
REDUCED 5p BOTTLES DE LATONNELL BRANDY
VODKA
WINE MERCHANTS
This Bar Loaned Free
14p

(*Opposite page*) illus. 87.
Swimming Pool Entrance (D091)

THE LIDO

This photograph of children waiting outside the entrance to the outdoor swimming pool in Great Malvern was one of the most popular in the exhibition in 2022. Two of the children were identified as brothers.

A photo of the swimming baths (called the Lido or the Swimming Pool) appears in several books of old photos of Malvern. Brian Iles, the local historian, believes that they were built around 1920 and said that they looked about the same forty years later. A Baths Committee appears in Stevens Directory for 1922. There were other outdoor swimming pools in the Malvern area, including one at British Camp and one at St Cuthberts in Malvern Link. Great Malvern baths were recalled with considerable, if sometimes shivering, fondness. Here are some 1970s memories.

Sean Austin remembered 'Our day out in Malvern'. After getting the train from Worcester to Great Malvern in the summer holidays, he and his friends spent the time climbing and playing on the hills.

> When we got back in to town it wasn't as much as going for shopping or anything else, as many people would now, but it was straight down to the Lido. I remember that the area where the Splash is now was an outdoor pool. And there was nothing better than on a hot summers day of literally dive-bombing

SWIMMING POOL
ADULTS
SWIMMING POOL
LAST TICKET SOLD
FOR THIS SESSION AT
POOL CLEARED AT
7-30. PM
CLOSED
CIGARETTES
EMBASSY

into cold frosty waters and spending as much time there until we got the train back to Worcester.

Gill Holt commented,

Happy days at Malvern open air swimming pool, where Splash is now. The sun cannot always have been shining but it seemed like that.

Her son Mike and daughter Emma added their experiences:

It always seemed to be cold in the water at Malvern lido, though that didn't stop me and my family – 3 sisters and mum and dad – swimming in the summer! I now go cold water swimming at 7 degrees, so I expect it was actually pretty warm, maybe even 19 degrees. My Dad used to teach other kids to dive from the side of the pool and I remember lots of them waiting in line! I remember diving down at the deep end and picking up coins we had thrown in and 'duck diving' also to pick them up. My oldest sister, Katie, was a better swimmer than me, but I tried to keep up. Dad used to dive off the top board and somersault, the only one as I remember. The boards were taken down as the pool was too shallow and it was too dangerous for a high board, just as well, I think. There were small opaque glass squares on the roof where you could sunbathe, and we looked through them into the changing rooms, seeing blurred shapes getting changed. Our family wore red polka dot bathrobes made by our mum,

Gillian, and lots of kids made comments and looked at us. I think I liked being different though.

Emma commented,

The swimming pool was only open in the summer. I learnt to swim there in 1967 in the small pool when I was five years old. I have a photo of myself in the pool at the time and have just noticed deck chairs around the side, which I don't remember. Maybe you had to pay to use them? I remember sitting on my towel on the paving slabs, usually leaning up against a wall. We went to the pool as a family, mum, dad and four children and had matching home-made white towelling robes with red spots/circles on them. We must have looked quite distinctive! We would often spend the whole afternoon or day there. We had a season ticket which was stamped with a star shape each time you went. There was a high diving board there at one time and my dad used to do somersault dives off it. At some point the high diving board was removed and replaced with a low springboard as the water was no longer considered deep enough for a board that high. I loved going there to swim and to sunbathe throughout my childhood and teenage years, particularly in the long hot summer of 1976.

I particularly remember the old-fashioned metal turnstiles at the entrance/exit and the upper sunbathing area which was directly above the changing rooms. There were sections of thick frosted glass tiles as well as paving stones on the sunbathing area which warmed up nicely in the sun. I enjoyed drying off by lying on them after a swim. You could see the movement of people in the changing rooms below, through the frosted glass tiles and when I was younger, I used to worry about being seen changing below. I certainly used to look down through the tiles, although you couldn't really see anything. Maybe the sunbathing area was built before the changing rooms were there, or perhaps the designer didn't think about it? I used to enjoy having a chocolate drink from a machine in the café after getting changed to go home. You could stand on a walkway outside the café while you were drinking it and watch the people who were still at the pool.

I left Malvern in the early 1980s when I was 18. I am now nearly 60 and still love swimming, especially in outdoor pools, but only if they are heated! It's a shame that the Malvern open air pool was demolished in the 1990s, but at least you can swim all year round at the Splash Leisure Pool which is there now.

And Jane Tinklin also remembered the pool,

The swimming pool was open air and you could sun bath on the roof of the building and splash about in the water, Rachel and Mum used to take us swimming when they could. It was easy walking distance from the restaurant which we ran. I remember a turnstile and the colour blue, which I assume was the tiling in the pool.

People have pointed out several features of the early seventies in the 1971 Lido photograph. Young boys tended to wear jeans or long trousers instead of short trousers worn in the sixties; whatever happened to duffle bags and how useful they were; and the first thing you saw when entering this healthy exercise area was a machine dispensing Embassy cigarettes!

The former Lido was demolished and soon replaced by Malvern Splash swimming pool and leisure complex. It was designed in 1989 by Charles Smith of Boston Spa with Abbey Henson Rowe Partnership and built on the edge of the park to provide better (and under cover) facilities with a range of popular fitness activities as well as swimming. It contrasted with other buildings in and next to the park with its square 'glitzy' panels in red painted frames. In 2021 Malvern Splash swimming pool was updated. The changing rooms have been refurbished, there are additional family changing areas and dedicated changing areas for people with disabilities. A new flume and wave machine have been installed. In 2022 Freedom Leisure who run the complex have carried out further improvements with new state-of-the-art facilities in the gym and cycling studio.[6]

6. www.freedom-leisure.co.uk

Games and Sports Equipment

(*Opposite page*) illus. 88. Park and Winter Gardens (D093)

THE SPORTS DEPOT, 12 CHURCH STREET

The shop in the same row as the Dorothy Café (*see illus. 24, D095*) sold many different kinds of sports and games equipment. Karen Hill remembered,

> The Sports Depot was a sports suppliers but, in the run up to bonfire night, they sold fireworks as did Hemingway's at Link Top which was a stationers and toy shop.

It was also an agent for several bicycle manufacturers. It stood in the row next to the Vacuum Sales and Servicing shop. The row has had several different occupants in recent years including Clark's shoe shop which closed not long ago and Mountain Warehouse which seemed ideally situated and was popular with hill walking visitors but transferred its business to the retail park. The Works which sells books, stationery and craft materials has survived the more recent changes. Newcomers include the attractive tapas café Bar Limon and the popular Weavers of Malvern Real Ale House.

Priory Park

THE PARK

The photograph used on the cover of the Malvern in a Day exhibition leaflet of 2022 shows a tranquil scene in the Park. A family group, of mum and dad with baby's pram near the rug and another group just beyond them further up the gentle grassy slope, the Priory and the Hills in the background. Look closely. On the edge of the rug on the left is a radio, just beyond is a football. People are sitting in deck chairs as if at the sea side.

A visitor to the Malvern in a Day exhibition said,

> You could hire a deck chair. They were kept stacked up at the side of the Winter Gardens. You could buy an ice-cream from the building just on the right, I think.

So perhaps not necessarily tranquil but on a nice day, more of a holiday atmosphere.

There was something missing from the park in 1971 compared with today. There was no bandstand. Today the bandstand is very much a focal point. In summer, a number of bands play different kinds of music and programmes here on Sunday afternoons. People visit to meet friends and listen to the music, sometimes sitting on the theatre steps. (There are no steps in the photo.) People also use the bandstand for other activities too. At various times during the week there are exercise groups, retired work colleagues getting together with flasks of coffee (useful during the Covid restrictions), and parents and young children playing. The mayor or another local VIP or organiser declares whatever function is being held in the park as 'open' from the bandstand and not long ago it provided a platform for speakers at the demonstration held to lobby in favour of the former Malvern Hills College being kept open and not being sold.

The bandstand looks old. It is a Grade II listed building. But in 1971 it stood in Victoria Park in Malvern Link where in fact it was originally listed in 1979. It was sited there after the end of the Second World War. Michael Dowty photographed it and the nearby children's playground.

It was later neglected and fell into disrepair. After lobbying by the Civic Society the bandstand was returned to the place it came from, having been built there originally in 1875. Pamela Hurle records in *Portrait of Malvern*,

> In Priory Park the old bandstand is now (1984) being re-erected in the place where it stood many years ago.

(*Above*) illus. 89. Save the College protest (JC62)

(*Opposite page*) illus. 90. Victoria Park Bandstand (D116)

(*Opposite page*) illus. 91. Priory Park Paddling Pool (089D)

The trees and shrubs in Priory Park remain. Now even more mature, they are famous for their variety and beauty – so many in such a comparatively small space. There are labels and leaflets about them and guided walks during Midsummer Malvern and other festivals. One visitor recalled another advantage of the park!

> I remember when I was about fourteen sneaking off for a smoke hidden by some of the bushes over there.

Michael Dowty took two photographs in 1971 of the park's amenities for young children. One shows workmen cleaning a round shallow pool with adjacent round sandpit early in the morning. The other shows children happily playing there later in the day. This photograph caught the attention of a little girl as she trotted along the wall outside Wilko during the 2022 exhibition. She was delighted to see a photo of children playing. Today there is a specially designed and built new play area with Flights of Fancy the provider of specialist play equipment and the surroundings by Avery Landscapes Ltd. What resulted is a unique, eco-friendly area with state-of-the-art items to swing, climb, run through and explore and children love it.

People still sit on the grass in the park. They bring their folding chairs or picnic blankets or sit on the benches provided alongside the paths, chat, read, listen to bands in the summer or simply watch the world go

(*Opposite page*) illus. 92. Boating pool (D090)

by. Icecream and drinks can be bought from visiting sales trolleys or from the cafe and taken to the terrace tables. On one very hot day in the summer of 2022, a visitor languidly reclined in a hammock he had hung between two trees. The park now sometimes hosts special events where stalls and awnings are set up selling, crafts or products. Other events include Science in the Park with activities based around many aspects of science and technology; Great Malvern Festival of Stories, a book fair for children; Midsummer Malvern events, hosted by the Civic Society. An event organised by Malvern Pride Committee was Pride in the Park with its rainbow flags and inclusive atmosphere attracting large crowds. The committee certainly achieved what they set out to:

> Our mission is to hold a free event for all to attend in Malvern to celebrate our differences.

This event could not have taken place in the seventies when same sex relationships were not routinely publicly recognised. Partners were not able to marry until 2014 although civil partnerships were recognised by law in 2004.

THE BOATING LAKE

The Swan Pool has been recently restored to provide a haven for nature. But in 1971 it was a boating lake. Jane Tinklin recalled:

The pond in Priory Park had paddle boats and canoes which you could hire. Part of the landing stage is still at the side of the pond. The boats were tied up at night on the island at the middle of the pond opposite the landing stage. The man running the boats sat in a deck chair and would call out the boats number when the time allowed was up.

In the 1870s the park had been the private grounds to the house, Priory Mansion, the home of a wealthy merchant, Albert Miles Speer. Now the Park is a place to be enjoyed by everyone. A volunteer group, the Friends of Priory Park, helps to maintain it.

Entertainment

MALVERN THEATRES (THE WINTER GARDENS)

The Dowty photo shows the Grange Road main entrance to the buildings with the different functions indicated. The buildings have been altered considerably over the years and at the time of writing the front part facing Grange Road is being rebuilt to provide better facilities for the community.

THE FESTIVAL THEATRE

The Festival Theatre held, as its name suggests, the Malvern Festival.

(Above) illus. 94. Rebuilding the theatre (JC100)

(Opposite page) illus. 93. Winter Gardens Entrance (D020)

This included the Shaw Festival, promoting George Bernard Shaw's plays. The premier of *The Apple Cart* and five other English or world premières directed by Barry Jackson in the '20s and '30s took place here. In 1971, it hosted a mixed programme including *On With the Dance: Ballet for All*, with dancers from the Royal Ballet. It also showed films. *The Lady Killers*, possibly the last of the great Ealing Comedies was screened in late July. Seats cost 30p or 25p, with pensioners only paying 5p. Today touring companies with different productions including plays pre- and post West-End runs offer a wide range of entertainment options. The theatre attracts audiences from many parts of the Midlands.

THE FORUM THEATRE

The Forum Theatre provides space for concerts, dance and productions requiring large or a flexible space without a proscenium arch. The youth theatre company uses part of the Forum for in-the-round productions.

Malvern Concert Club, founded by Elgar, holds chamber music concerts here often with international visiting performers.

DEVELOPMENTS AT THE THEATRE COMPLEX

The current alterations are to provide space for further uses by building a new workshop space and rehearsal studio to increase participation opportunities for people of all ages and abilities in our community.

The recent (January 2023) award to the Theatre Complex following a successful bid to the government's Levelling Up Fund will allow for further exciting developments. An outdoor amphitheatre, for example, is quoted in the *Gazette* as 'one of the stand out proposals'. At present, the theatre complex is staying open throughout the current alterations.

The premises of other theatres were here in 1971 but were not used as theatres:

THE COACH HOUSE THEATRE

The Coach House was originally part of the Grange property. It was saved from demolition in 1984 and is now Grade II listed. Used for some time as a scenery store, it was extended to form a theatre in 2004–5 and bought from the District Council in 2014. It is now owned by Coach House Theatre, a registered charity, and has been developed as a community arts venue. The theatre is equipped to professional standards and provides space for smaller scale productions in an intimate space.

Illus. 95. Hall Bros. Ltd. (D068)

Avril Rowland's play Shakespeare's Second-Best Bed was a fairly recent good example of how a solo actor's performance can work so well here. It also provides opportunities for children to develop their skills and a space for talks (not long ago on A. E. Housman, the Bromsgrove-born poet). The French Cinema Club is based here too with regular opportunities to see classic films.

Two unique famous venues of the past are worth mentioning, although neither were here in the Seventies in their original form.

On Foley House (now apartments and previously as in the photograph the premises of Hall's building business) on Worcester Road a plaque records the presence of the theatre of the famous Lanchester Marionettes. The theatre could seat fifty people and was a great success in the Malvern Festival in the 1930s attracting attention of a wide audience and the admiration of George Bernard Shaw whose last play, Shakes v Shaw, was commissioned by the Arts Council in 1949. The theatre had provided sophisticated entertainment and the marionettes were intricately made by Waldo Lanchester for the productions. One of his creations is displayed in Malvern Museum. The Lanchesters moved to Stratford on Avon in 1951 where they established the Puppet Centre following the sale of Foley House in Malvern. They had been hugely successful, entertaining the troops during the Second World War and touring in the UK, including appearing at the Edinburgh Festival.

The other theatre was on a very much smaller scale and was created by another puppet enthusiast Denis Neal in 1999. A former public loo in Edith Walk became the Theatre of Small Convenience. You can find more information in chapter five, Public Services.

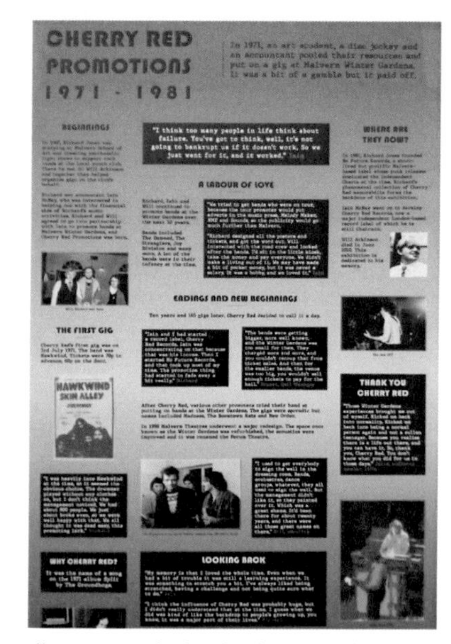

Illus. 96 Poster displayed in the Forum Theatre (JC124)

THE BANDS

Gill Holt whose series of oral history books provides a wealth of information about Malvern life emphasised the importance of the bands at the Winter Gardens around the time of the Dowty photos. She said:

> That was the big thing about the 1970s.

And for very many, it certainly was. In the late 1960s Freddy Bannister and Severn Promotions were the main promoters and bands including The Who, Pink Floyd and Jethro Tull appeared in Malvern. A flick through the pages of the *Gazette* for 1971 reveals that among the wrestling and ballroom dancing (licenced bar-buffet-chicken-in-a-basket) events were a number of bands which continued to attract the young of Malvern and beyond.

Plastic Dog music promoters from Bristol started booking acts in 1970 (Derek and the Dominos, Eric Clapton's band), and continued with others through to 1972. In 1971 local art student Richard Jones with Will Atkins, DJ, and Ian McNay, an accountant, formed Cherry Red Promotions and at the start of July, became one of the main promoters

Illus. 97. Archive project: Juke Box (JC)

with the band Hawkwind, with Skin Alley the supporting act, as their first gig. Tickets cost 60p in advance from the box office or the Music Centre in Worcester, or 70p at the door. They attracted an audience of 800. Hawkwind, just a month before, had appeared at the second Glastonbury Festival, at the time a free event. Cherry Red continued their Malvern promotions for 10 years. They went on to develop the Cherry Red Records label. Other bands which appeared in 1971 included Mott the Hoople, Juicy Lucy, Skid Row, Super Tramp. The bands were, said Richard Jones in 2018,

> The backdrop to people's growing up . . . a major part of their life.

You can hear an extract from his interview on the website below. The introduction to the archive sums it up.

> The rock music performances at the Winter Gardens are part of the rich musical heritage of Malvern, and indeed the West Midlands. We believe that if a proper record is not made of them now, then in a generations time they will be forgotten.

The excitement of these days has been captured by the archive project now available at www.malvernrockarchive.org.uk.

A few years ago an exhibition was held at Malvern Library where you could listen to a juke box and read posters with lots of information about the bands and promoters of the gigs. The posters are now on display in a ground floor corridor to the Forum Theatre and can be seen when the theatre is open for performances. The juke box is in Malvern Library where you can use it to listen to first-hand accounts of these exciting times.

Carnival Records in Church Street buy and sell new and used vinyl records so is worth checking their website for favourite bands.

THE CINEMA

The cinema had its origins in the picture house, 'talkies' being available from the 1930s. In 1971, the cinema was still very popular. Michael Dowty has a photograph advertising the film of the musical *Hello Dolly*, certificate U. Other films shown in July 1971 were the *Quiller Memorandum* (A), *Where Eagles Dare* (A) with Richard Burton, the film of *Dad's Army* (U), *Take a Girl Like You* (X) and *Percy* with Hywel Bennett and Britt Ekland (X). Seats cost 30p, 35p or 45p with reductions for children and OAPs (old age pensioners, as pensioners were then called.) The British Board of Film Classification reviewed the earlier classification system and introduced the AA certificate in 1970. U certificates were given for films for general exhibition, A indicated parental guidance required for children under twelve, AA strong adult content – the viewer had to be fourteen years old at least – and X meant explicit content for public exhibition when no one under eighteen was present.

Jane Tinklin described the cinema:

In the cinema you had to go up the red carpeted stairs to buy a ticket and the door into the stalls was opposite the box office and the stairs to the balcony were just to the right of the ticket office.

Michael Dowty's photograph of the front of the Winter Gardens shows that an information office was also located there.

Home Entertainment

OXLEY'S, 18 CHURCH STREET

Jane Tinklin recalled,

> There was a music shop in what is now one half of the Oxfam Shop (the other half was vacant but had previously been Quality Dry Cleaners).

The photo of Oxley's window shows us one of the most popular venues for young people in Malvern who flocked to the rock concerts at the Winter Gardens. Records of the bands' music could be listened to before being bought in the shop which was presided over by 'Ma' Oxley. The shop also sold a wide range of records and record players from HMV and Columbia. Long playing records (LPs) and singles were on sale. In July in 1971 LPs were on special offer and cost between 73p and £1.45 each. Oxley's also sold musical instruments and had a piano workshop.

RECORDS
OXLEY'S
"HIS MASTER'S VOICE AND COLUMBIA
GRAMOPHONES AND RECORDS
SPECIAL
Make Sure
GIVE
EMI
KAREN YOUNG

(*Above*) illus. 99. Burston and Co. Hacker Radio (D159)

(*Opposite page*) illus. 98. Oxley's Music Shop (D157)

Of the mid-70s David Williamson wrote:

> We were looking for a piano for our house. We were advised to go to Oxley's and I remember the shop front and premises behind linked to Cecilia Hall. There seemed to be a lot of pianos for sale then and Oxley's had several for purchase. We bought a Lipp of Stuttgart upright and still have it now (2021).

Records were also sold at Woolworths and Roger Hales remembered the shop his mother once ran in Malvern Link.

> My mother worked. She ran a little record shop at the rear of the premises. People say to me very often now, contemporaries of mine, 'Oh I remember coming to your shop and buying my Beatles records or my Elvis records.' And I know if a record was in short supply, Beatles and Presley always were, she'd never let me have a record until she'd supplied all her better customers.

BURSTON'S, 105 CHURCH STREET

Burston's business was in the Exchange at the corner of Graham Road in 1971 where Rhubarb Home is now. The photograph shows radios but Burston's sold a range of electrical goods including cassette recorders and TVs. TVs could be rented at 9/6 a week according to newspaper adverts in January 1971, 45p after decimal currency was introduced in February that year. Portable radios were popular with young people although the breakthrough came with the real portability of the Sony Walkman in 1979. Cassette recorders became popular in the 1970s and one of Phillips models cost £28.35 in 1971. Blank cassettes cost from 50p for a 60-minute tape. Calculators started to become available at the end of the year.

There is a clue to Rhubarb Home's original use facing you as you enter the shop. A tiled mural with its fishing boats has been uncovered and shows that this was once a fish shop. The owner Mr William 'Fishy' Davis had supplied fish and poultry in Malvern for twenty years and in 1901 he decided to branch out and build a number of shops on the corner of Church Street and Graham Road and commissioned local architect Albert C. Baker to design the Exchange. Exchanges have been called the forerunners of the modern office block with shops below, offices and apartments above. The corner plot had formerly been occupied by Malvern Cottage. The original shop opened in March 1902. It had windows which opened out to provide a stall on to Church Street and downstairs the basement was lined with tiles to keep the stock cool.

Illus. 100. Fishing boat tile mural in Rhubarb Home (JC. Courtesy of Nigel Morris, Rhubarb Home)

Radio and Television History

Burston's window in Michael Dowty's photo is dominated by transistor radios. In 1967 the BBC had up until then broadcast the Home Service, the Light Programme and the Third programme. Pop music was available firstly on Radio Luxemburg and then on pirate radio stations which were operated from ships in international waters e.g. Radio Caroline. The Marine Broadcasting Offences Act made the immensely popular pirate radio illegal. The BBC created Radio 1 using many of the well-known former pirate DJs including Tony Blackburn and Kenny Everett. Opened on 30 September 1967, young people now had a much more informal BBC channel they could relate to. At the same time the other channels were re-badged. The Home Service became Radio 4, The Light Programme Radio 2, and the Third Programme Radio 3. So by 1971 ownership of radios was influenced by the channel revamps and Radio 1. The availability of small portable radios no longer restricted households to one or two radios plugged in to the mains.

Television also changed in the late '60s. Then the three channels were BBC1, BBC2 and ITV. In 1967 colour television was launched on BBC2 initially, with the expectation of its availability on BBC1 and ITV in London and the Midlands by the end of 1969. The limited launch was partly due to the transmitters needed and partly because it was uncertain how quickly people would buy or rent new television sets. The *Radio Times*, 29 June 1967 included a question-and-answer section for viewers. Here are two examples:

> Q. Will I need a special set? A. Black and white sets cannot be converted to receive colour. But you can get black and white programmes on a colour set.

And

> Q. Do I need an additional licence for colour? A. There will be an additional fee of £5. The Postmaster General is to announce when it will be payable.

Early colour programmes were *One Pair of Eyes*, *Impact*, *Late Night Line Up* and the western, *The Virginian*. The full service was to start on 2 December with BBC 2 having 80 per cent of its programmes in colour. David Attenborough was controller of BBC2. He wrote in the *Radio Times* in 1967,

> Many viewers are no doubt waiting to make up their minds about colour until they see it with their own eyes.

Four years later the *Malvern Gazette* had adverts from Burston's, Hales, Wireless Supply and Mercian Radio for colour televisions either to buy (expensive) or to rent.

John Life of Worcester advertised an

> ITT-KB colour TV for sale £238 plus £4.70 for a stand to put it on.

From Ralph Hales of Malvern:

[a] colour TV (leading brands) rental £6.25 per month, installed for £18.75 down payment with no more to pay for three months.

A black and white set cost from 40p per week.

While several companies advertised colour televisions for sale, the price was not always mentioned. It would usually depend on the size of screen required (19, 22 or 25 inch) and purchase might mean a visit to the shop to see the range of televisions available .

A new transmitter which would boost the signal from Sutton Coldfield was put up in Malvern to bring 'better colour TV reception'. An article heralding the news and surrounded by adverts for colour TV appeared in the *Gazette* in November 1971. Hopefully sales and rentals of colour would benefit from the run up to Christmas.

Illus. 101. The new transmitter (Courtesy of *Malvern Gazette*)

Roger Hales, Ralph Hales son, recalled the early days of his father's business.

> After being demobbed from the RAF he started his business in Malvern Link. He grew it through hard work and personal contact. The phone would ring in the evening and they would say 'my televisions broken down'. My dad would go out and repair it. When I asked him why he did that, he said that was because if I give people good service, they will stay with me.

Some of the most popular programmes in 1971 are still referred to and sometimes repeated today. The Two Ronnies which first went out on 10 April was an 'immediate success' and ran until 1988 with Ronnie Barker and Ronnie Corbett. Michael Parkinson's chat show started on 19 June. It had an eleven-year run followed by a revival for six years in the 1990s. In October the Generation Game started with Bruce Forsyth and its famous conveyor belt of gifts to be memorised and won.

There was no internet in 1971 although later Queen Elizabeth II on a visit to the Royal Radar Establishment in Malvern in 1976 sent her first email via ARPANET, the forerunner of the World Wide Web, defined by Tim Berners Lee in 1990. Home computers started to appear in 1977 with a number of companies developing products. In the UK in 1980 Sir Clive Sinclair introduced the ZX80 with competition from Amstrad and Commodore. Atari arcade games appeared in the late 70s.

The BBC programmes about technology, Tomorrow's World, showed its audience what the future might bring with items about the first computers in home and work place (1967), ATMs for access to money (1969), a phone that is mobile (1979) and the dawn of the information superhighway (1994). The BBC Microcomputer (built by Acorn) was designed for use in education and came into use in schools in the 1980s and for many people it was the first computer they used.

Conclusion

The photographs taken by Michael Dowty in 1971 and the memories of people of the late sixties and early seventies highlight the differences between the way people lived then and today. The 1970s saw some major changes and in some ways the time around 1971 seems to have been a bridge between the more relaxed society of the sixties and what was to follow in the following decade. Today in the first quarter of the 21st century the influence of the spread of information technology, made possible by developments in the sixties (transistors and microchips), underpins our society and has changed the way people live in so many ways. The Covid pandemic could not have been predicted in 1971. It too is having a lasting effect on how we run our lives. A greater awareness of environmental issues is turning the tide of consumerism – no longer do we hear the phrases of 'built in obsolescence' or 'fantastic plastic'. Instead people seek out the green credentials of those supplying us with the necessities of life.

I have mentioned many changes, some not just in the seventies, in the different chapters of the book. Here is a summary.

The Common Market and whether Britain should join was often discussed in the national and local press, including the *Malvern Gazette*, in 1971. The EEC and EU developed with Britain as a member but the membership ended with Brexit and now other allegiances and suppliers of goods are being explored and relationships developed. Locally, supermarkets were much smaller in the 1970s and while we have seen the recent closure of two large shops and, before this, the building of the retail park, we have also had the arrival of Waitrose which attracts shoppers from Great Malvern itself and from further afield. Iceland has a good home delivery service and selection of frozen and fresh foods and other necessities. There are fewer small food shops but a couple of convenience stores and two specialist shops, the Bran Tub and Green Link provide well for those who prefer organic produce or have special dietary needs. Cafés and restaurants too provide plenty of choice. Wilko has a wide range of household and personal goods from cosmetics to stationery and items for the garden.

Illus. 102. Waitrose building site 1999 (JC collection)

There is probably a better selection of small, locally based shops than in many towns. Visitors often remark positively on this aspect in local surveys.

There has been a growth in the number of charity shops in more recent years, selling good quality clothes, furniture, household goods and books, all attractively displayed.

Better home laundry facilities have led to the disappearance of dry cleaners (although Waitrose has a dry cleaning and laundry service in association with Johnsons the Cleaners). The long established shoe repair shop as shown in the photograph has recently closed in Great Malvern but has a branch in Barnards Green. Shoes can now be recycled in the large bins found in car parks, where unwanted clothes and fabrics can also be deposited. There is a large recycling centre not far from the retail park where people can take items no longer needed.

Local government changes were discussed in 1971 and for a time it was thought that Malvern may become the administrative centre for Hereford and Worcester. Although the centre didn't materialise, for a while the counties operated as one local authority. They are now individual counties once more. Malvern is in Worcestershire with the county boundary nearby. It has a District Council which takes in some smaller towns and villages and shares some back-office functions with neighbouring Wychavon District Council at Pershore. There is also a town council for more local matters. The county council based in Worcester is responsible for infra structure. It also runs the library service which is based at the Hive along with archives, archaeology and the joint university and public library. The library in Malvern itself has changed in many ways. IT services provide access to a huge range of information resources and enable users to work in the library itself or from home. Many community activities take place there, there is a small café and premises are provided for the local job centre and an office for the registrar.

Newspaper deliveries have all but disappeared but printed newspaper sales at shops and supermarkets still seem to be popular, although many prefer to get their news on-line from a computer, from TV channels or via mobile phones. The choice of home or on the move entertainment and communications (now written, spoken and visual) with friends, family, businesses and organisations, or with complete strangers, and by a range of social media continues to develop as technological possibilities are explored and exploited.

The closure of high street banks has been one of the more obvious recent changes in the town centre with the development of on-line banking from home, especially during the Covid regulations and lockdowns, and the decline in the need for cash – a great contrast between now and the introduction of decimal currency in 1971.

Public transport is comparatively good but there is less access to nearby areas for those without cars and the lack of bus services in the evenings cuts down choices for some. Train services are still fast and comparatively good to Hereford, Worcester and Birmingham and it is possible to get to London and Oxford fairly easily too. Electric vehicles are becoming more popular and there are charging points in several car parks. Parking is still an issue for some and traffic is sometimes briefly delayed because of delivery vans and road works.

There has been a noticeable trend towards service businesses in the town with a recent growth in the number and variety of places to eat

Illus. 103. Malvern Community Hospital 2021 (RS, Malvern Civic Society. A day in Malvern)

and drink. The number of hairdressers, barbers and nail-bars (the latter unheard of in 1971) has grown. The theatre continues to thrive and develop and attracts visitors from a wide area with its varied programmes.

On the energy front, Natural Gas was introduced in 1971 but now environmental concerns over power generation and climate change have become major issues. Nationally alternative sources of energy, including solar, wind, hydrogen and the expansion of nuclear are being explored and some homes in Malvern have solar panels on their roof tops. Some fields in the area now contain solar panels which produce energy for the national grid. Concerns over energy costs to businesses, agriculture and households are increasingly important. Energy is now provided by private companies.

The hills here do not have wind turbines. Managed by the Malvern Hills Trust, they continue to be a major attraction for local people and visitors alike. Open spaces are considered increasingly important for good physical and mental health and those who live here are fortunate in having not just the hills but parks and commons close to their homes. There may no longer be a lido but Malvern Splash is available for swimming and other forms of indoor exercise.

If residents need medical treatment, Malvern people still have a community hospital for minor injuries but for major health concerns doctors refer them to Redditch, Kidderminster or Worcester where specialist diagnosis and treatment is available. The National Health Service is still recovering from the effects of the pandemic on it and waiting lists and staffing issues continue to be a concern nationally.

The sense of community in Malvern is strong. There are many groups covering all kinds of interests. There is never 'nothing to do'!

When John McWhirter came to live in Malvern in 1973 to work as a scientist at the Royal Radar Establishment, he was enthusiastic about what he found.

> I absolutely loved the town. I couldn't believe that I had found something quite so attractive and so congenial and with really good science labs . . . I came to get the local paper – the *Gazette* they said comes out on a Thursday and very little accommodation comes up to rent. I rang a chap up and he said to come round this evening. I wondered if I would get it. This was the garden flat at St Andrew's House next to the Library. Brilliant. Super Accommodation. I agreed right away to take it. When we moved here it was a beautiful autumn – the 'Indian Summer' went on for a week . . .

Great Malvern was recently included in the *Sunday Times* Best Places to live list, sponsored by the Halifax. Not surprisingly this was reported in the *Gazette* (MG24/3/2023) with the comment from a local councillor about the strong retail sector of the town centre and the strong sense of community.

I hope that this book with the photographs and the memories of

Malvern people has presented an opportunity to look at aspects of life around the early seventies and some of the ways people lived in the not-too-distant past, and to think of how and why things have changed. Perhaps the only certainty is that change is here to stay – a trite saying which in one form or another goes back at least as far as the Ancient Greeks!

AUSTIN & Co
SOLO

(*Opposite page*) illus. 104.
New shops at Brays building 2021
(RS – Malvern Civic Society. A Day in Malvern)

Acknowledgements

Lots of people have been involved in this work and my thanks go to them all.

The work to catalogue, conserve and make available the photographs is a partnership involving primarily the Friends of Malvern Museum whose volunteers are carrying out the work on this and other collections, Niru Fallon, and the staff of Malvern Library where the Dowty collection is held along with other historic resources, Bridget and Fiona Dowty (the copyright owners) and everyone who has contributed their memories. Others have given advice, expertise, funds, and support. Thanks also go to businesses and shop staff who have been kind enough to answer questions and discuss their premises and those who have provided illustrations and access to their archives. Special thanks go to Faith Renger, Cora Weaver, Rosemary Preece, Brian Iles, Ian Thompson, Stephen Goodenough, Dr. James Herring and Colin Banks for their expertise, encouragement and advice. They have contributed material, supplied and digitized photographs, read my text, helped with IT issues and simply been there when I needed someone to check what I was doing. Thanks also go to Malvern Civic Society, Malvern Town Council, Malvern Hills District Council for financial support for the initial project.

Sources of the illustrations provided are indicated in the captions:

D = Michael Dowty

RS = Robert Savage (via Malvern Civic Society)

JC = Jan Condon

Names of the contributors to the MID oral history project are given in the text.

And finally, thanks go to the staff at Aspect Design without whose skill and experience this book would have not been possible.

Sources of Information

GOAD'S PLAN

A major source of information for this book was Goad's Plan of Malvern, March 1971 available in the reference section of Malvern Library. The plan is one of several of different dates held by the library and of a series produced for many British town centres, showing mostly retail premises and streets. The original Goad plans were developed in the nineteenth century by a company in Canada set up by British-born Charles Goad to produce plans to enable insurance companies to estimate fire-risk. There was later a branch in London. In the 1960s the plans evolved to concentrate on shopping centre and town centre development. Goad is now owned by Experian.

For more information see: the National Library of Scotland and Hull History Centre websites. (Search dates 23/2/2023.) https://nls.uk/towns/Goad/info.html and https://hullhistorycentre.org.uk/research/research-guides/goad-maps.aspx

The author at work consulting a Goad's plan.

Bibliography

Allison, Ronald (1980) *The Country Life Book of Britain in the Seventies*. London, Hamlyn Publishing Group.

Briggs, Asa (1994) *A Social History of England: from Ice Age to the Channel Tunnel*. London, BCA by arrangement Weidenfeld and Nicolson.

Brooks, Alan and Pevsner, Nikolaus (2007, reprinted with corrections 2016) *Buildings of England: Worcestershire*. New Haven and London, Yale University Press.

Butt, Stephen (2018) *British Retail and the Men Who Shaped It*. Barnsley, Pen and Sword Books.

Byers, Anthony (1981) *Centenary of Service: a History of Electricity in the Home*. London, The Electricity Council.

Cockayne, Steve (2018) *Master of the Marionettes: the Life and Work of Waldo Lanchester*. Glasgow, The Scottish Mask and Puppet Centre.

Davidson, Louisa (2016) *An Architectural Guidebook: Great Malvern, Worcestershire*. Worcester, Historic Environment Record Buildings of Worcestershire Project.

Dowty, Michael (1988) *Worcester in a Day*. Gloucester, Alan Sutton Publishing.

Endeavour London Ltd (2010) T*he '70s in Pictures*. London, Exclusive Editions and Marks and Spencer plc.

Ewing, Elizabeth (1978) *Dress and Undress: a History of Women's Underwear*. London, Batsford.

Harcup, John Winsor (2010) *The Malvern Water Cure: Victims for Weeks in Wet Sheets*. Great Malvern, Capella Archive.

Hobbs, Tony (2012) *The Pubs of the Malverns, Upton and Nearby Villages*. Almeley, Longaston Press.

Hockney, David and Gayford, Martin (new edition. 2020). *A History of Pictures: From the Cave to the Computer Screen*. London. Thames and Hudson.

Hurle, Pamela and Winsor, John (1985) *Portrait of Malvern*. London and Chichester, Phillimore.

Iles, Brian (2005) *Images of England: The Malverns*. Stroud, Tempus Publishing.

Iles, Brian (2009) *Malvern Through Time*. Stroud, Amberley Publishing.

Lound, Andrew P. B. (2017) *RMS Titanic: Made in the Midlands*. Stroud, The History Press.

Lucas, J. W. (1940) *History of Malvern Library*. Malvern, Malvern Library.

Malvern Gazette and Ledbury Reporter (1971) 2 vols.

Malvern District Council (1972) 'Annual Reports of the Medical Officer of Health and the Chief Public Health Inspector for the Year 1971'.

Marwick, Arthur (1996) *British Society Since 1945*. London, Penguin Books.

Mitra, Barbara M. and Johnson, Rachel E. (Eds) (2015) *Gender Construction in Kays Catalogues 1920 to the New Millennium*. Cambridge, Cambridge Academic.

Mulkeen, Patrick (2022) *Radio Times: The Sixties*. London, Ben Head/Immediate Company.

Pelik, Rowena A. (1983) *C. W. Dyson Perrins: a Brief Account of His Life, His Achievements, His Collections and Benefactions*. Worcester, Dyson Perrins Museum Trust.

Seatter, Robert (2022) *Broadcasting Britain: 100 Years of the BBC*. London, Dorling Kindersley.

Sked, Alan and Cook, Chris (1993) *Post-war Britain: a Political History*. London, Penguin Books.

Smith, Brian (1964) *A History of Malvern*. Leicester, Leicester University Press.

Starling, Boris with Bradbury, David (2020) *The Official History of Britain: Our Story in Numbers as Told by the National Statistical Office*. London, Harper Collins.

Stewart, Susan (2020) *Painted Faces: A Colourful History of Cosmetics*.

Stroud, Amberley Publishing.

Tambrini, Michael (1991) *The Look of the Century*. London, Dorling Kindersley.

Trepte, Sally (2022) *Warwick House of Malvern and Gertrude Mitchell the Woman Who Created It*. Malvern, Aspect Design.

Weaver, Cora and Osborne, Bruce (1994) *Aquae Malvernensis*. Malvern, Cora Weaver.

Ziegler, Philip (1986) *Elizabethan Britain 1926–1986*. London, Hamlyn Publishing Group.

Ziegler, Philip (1999) *The Francis Frith Collection: Britain Then and Now*. London, Weidenfeld and Nicolson.

WEBSITES

British Social Attitudes Survey www.bea.natien.ac.uk

Malvern Gazette www.malverngazette.co.uk

Malvern Rock Archive www.malvernrockarchive.org.uk

Retrowow www.retrowow.co.uk

Tate Gallery www.tate.org.uk/art/images

Victoria and Albert Museum www.vam.ac.uk/articles/sixrevolutionary-designs-by-mary-quant

Whitworth Gallery www.whitworth.manchester.ac.uk/collections

THE FOLLOWING BOOKS WHICH MAKE EXTENSIVE USE OF ORAL HISTORY SOURCES WERE CONSULTED:

Barnards Green History Group (2017) *Barnard's Green Then and Now: a History of Barnard's Green Shopping Area*. Malvern, Barnards Green History Group.

Bramford, Margaret (2000) *This Was Our Malvern! Vol 1. Malvern Link*. Margaret Bramford.

Friends of Croome Park led by Eileen Clement *Croome Before the National Trust: the Friends of Croome Park Oral History Project*. National Trust.

Guarlford History Group (2005) *The Guarlford Story*. Malvern, Guarlford History Group.

Herring, James E. (2020) *Dunbar in the 1950s: Rationing, Housing, Entertainment, Shops and Shopping*. Dunbar, Dunbar and District History Society.

Holt, Gill (ed) (2005) *Malvern Voices: Work and Leisure: an Oral History*. Malvern, Malvern Museum.

Payne-Lunn, Sheena (2nd ed. 2023) *Worcester Life Stories in the Words of Local People*. Worcester, Worcester City Historic Environment Record.